DEFENDING ISRAEL

WITHDRAWN

ALSO BY MARTIN VAN CREVELD

Moshe Dayan

Das Bevorzugte Geschlecht

Men, Women and War

The Art of War: War and Military Thought

The Rise and Decline of the State

The Encyclopaedia of Revolutions and Revolutionaries from A to Z (ed.)

The Sword and the Olive: A History of the Israel Defense Force

Airpower and Maneuver Warfare

Nuclear Proliferation and the Future of Conflict

The Transformation of War

The Training of Officers: From Professionalism to Irrelevance

Technology and War: 2000 B.C. to the Present

Command in War

Fighting Power: German and U.S. Army Performance, 1939–1945

Supplying War: Logistics from Wallenstéin to Patton

Hitler's Strategy, 1940–1941: The Balkan Clue

THOMAS DUNNE BOOKS ⚑ ST. MARTIN'S GRIFFIN
NEW YORK

DEFENDING ISRAEL

A CONTROVERSIAL PLAN
TOWARD PEACE

MARTIN VAN CREVELD

THOMAS DUNNE BOOKS.
An imprint of St. Martin's Press.

Design by Gretchen Achilles

Maps by Mark Stein Studios

www.stmartins.com

Library of Congress Cataloging-in-Publication Data

Van Creveld, Martin L.
    Defending Israel : a strategic plan for peace and security / Martin van Creveld.
        p. cm.
    Includes bibliographical references (p. 167) and index (p. 183).
    ISBN 0-312-32866-4 (hc)
    ISBN 0-312-32867-2 (pbk)
    EAN 978-0-312-32867-2
    1. Arab-Israeli conflict. 2. Israel—Defenses. 3. Israel—Military policy. 4. Israel—Boundaries—Arab countries. 5. Arab countries—Boundaries—Israel. I. Title.

UA853.I8 V37297 2004
355'.03305694—dc22   2004059343

First St. Martin's Griffin Edition: September 2005

10 9 8 7 6 5 4 3 2 1

CONTENTS

*The fact that everybody believes in something
does not always prove it is true. If anything, the contrary.*

—FRIEDRICH NIETZSCHE

MAP 1. ISRAEL AND THE MIDDLE EAST.

ISRAEL AND THE
MIDDLE EAST

© 2004, Mark Stein Studios

MAP 2. ISRAEL, GAZA, AND THE WEST BANK (PRE-1967).

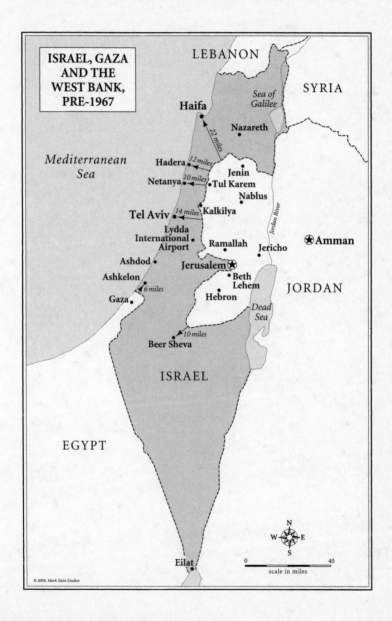

ISRAEL, GAZA
AND THE
WEST BANK,
PRE-1967

LEBANON

SYRIA

*Sea of
Galilee*

Haifa

Nazareth

22 miles

*Mediterranean
Sea*

Hadera *12 miles*

Jenin

Netanya *10 miles* **Tul Karem**

Nablus

Tel Aviv *14 miles* **Kalkilya**

Jordan River

**Lydda
International
Airport**

Ramallah

Jericho

⊛**Amman**

Ashdod

Jerusalem⊛

Ashkelon

6 miles

**Beth
Lehem**

JORDAN

Gaza

Hebron

*Dead
Sea*

10 miles

Beer Sheva

ISRAEL

EGYPT

N
W ✦ E
S

0   40
scale in miles

Eilat

© 2004, Mark Stein Studios

MAP 3. ISRAEL AND THE TERRITORIES (POST-1967 WAR).

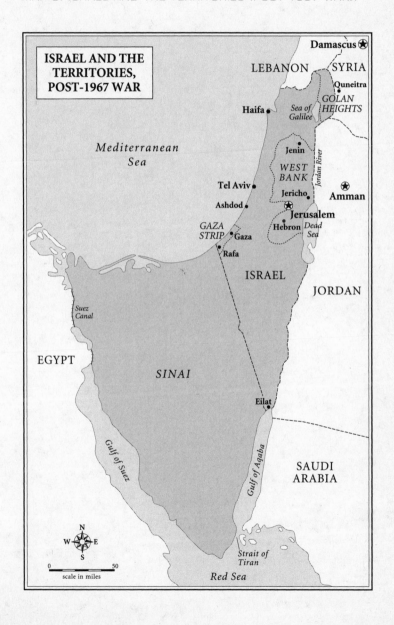

ISRAEL AND THE TERRITORIES, POST-1967 WAR

Damascus ✪

LEBANON   SYRIA

Quneitra

GOLAN HEIGHTS

Haifa ●   *Sea of Galilee*

Mediterranean Sea

Jenin ●

WEST BANK

Tel Aviv ●   Jericho ●   ✪ Amman

Ashdod ●   ✪ Jerusalem

GAZA STRIP ● Gaza   Hebron ● *Dead Sea*

● Rafa

ISRAEL   JORDAN

Suez Canal

EGYPT

SINAI

Eilat ●

Gulf of Suez

Gulf of Aqaba

SAUDI ARABIA

N
W ✦ E
S

0 _____ 50
scale in miles

Strait of Tiran

Red Sea

MAP 4. SECURITY ARRANGEMENTS IN THE SINAI (POST-1980).

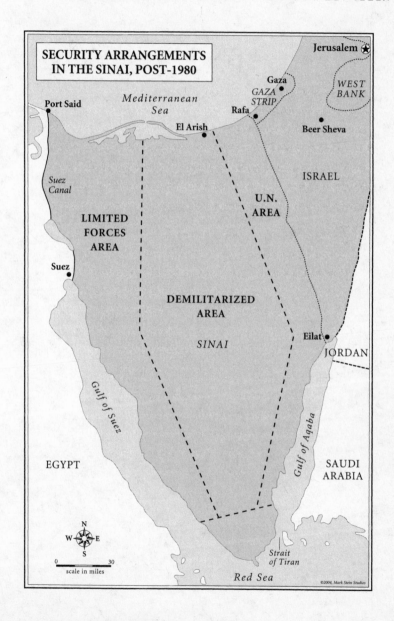

SECURITY ARRANGEMENTS
IN THE SINAI, POST-1980

MAP 5. CROSS SECTION OF THE HOLY LAND.

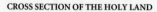
CROSS SECTION OF THE HOLY LAND

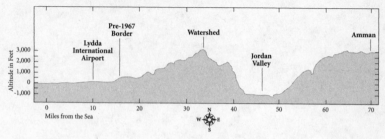

MAP 6. STRATEGIC ROADS IN THE WEST BANK.

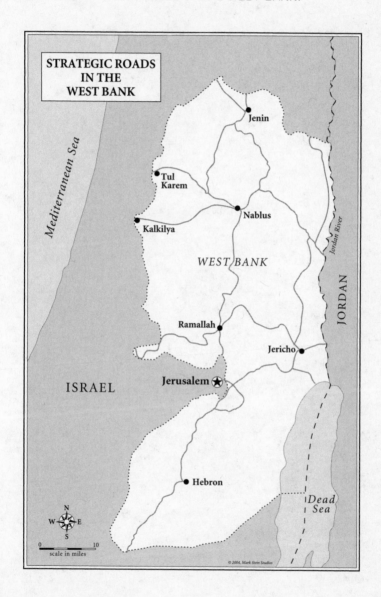

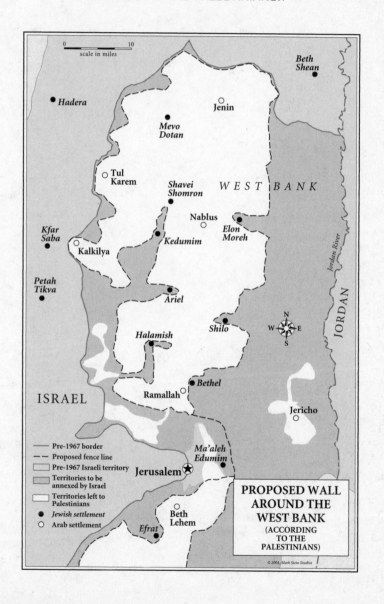

0   10
scale in miles

Beth
Shean

Hadera

Jenin

Mevo
Dotan

Tul
Karem

WEST BANK

Shavei
Shomron

Nablus

Elon
Moreh

Kfar
Saba

Kedumim

Kalkilya

Petah
Tikva

Ariel

Jordan River

JORDAN

Halamish

Shilo

N
W   E
S

Bethel

Ramallah

Jericho

ISRAEL

Pre-1967 border
Proposed fence line
Pre-1967 Israeli territory
Territories to be
annexed by Israel
Territories left to
Palestinians
● Jewish settlement
○ Arab settlement

Ma'aleh
Edumim

Jerusalem ★

**PROPOSED WALL
AROUND THE
WEST BANK**
(ACCORDING
TO THE
PALESTINIANS)

Beth
Lehem

Efrat

© 2004 Mark Stein Studios

MAP 8. THE GAZA STRIP.

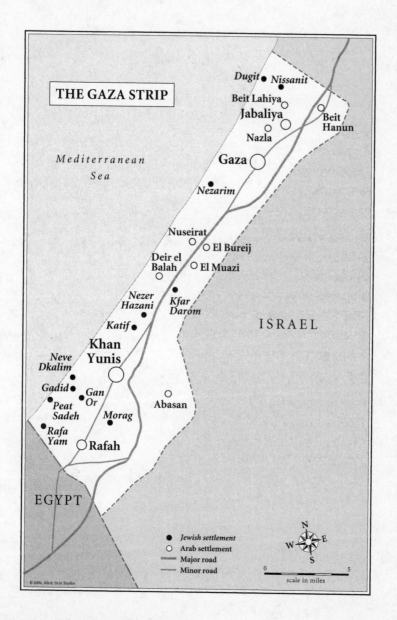

THE GAZA STRIP

Dugit • Nissanit
Beit Lahiya ○
Jabaliya ○
○ Beit Hanun
Nazla ○

Mediterranean Sea

Gaza ○

Nezarim •

Nuseirat ○
○ El Bureij
Deir el Balah
○ El Muazi
○

Nezer Hazani •
Kfar Darom •
Katif •

ISRAEL

Khan Yunis ○

Neve Dkalim •
Gadid •
Gan Or •
• Peat Sadeh
Abasan ○
Morag •
Rafa Yam •
○ Rafah

EGYPT

• Jewish settlement
○ Arab settlement
—— Major road
—— Minor road

N
W E
S

0 _____ 5
scale in miles

© 2004, Mark Stein Studios

MAP 9. JERUSALEM.

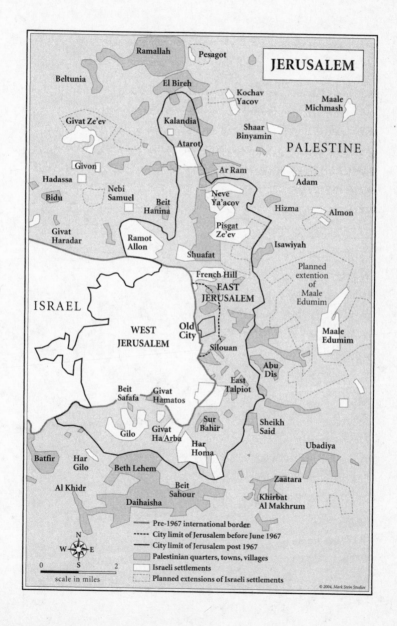

JERUSALEM

Ramallah
Pesagot
Beltunia
El Bireh
Kochav
Yacov
Maale
Michmash
Givat Ze'ev
Kalandia
Shaar
Binyamin
Atarot
PALESTINE
Givon
Ar Ram
Hadassa
Adam
Nebi
Bidu
Samuel
Beit
Neve
Hanina
Ya'acov
Hizma
Almon
Pisgat
Ze'ev
Givat
Haradar
Ramot
Allon
Isawiyah
Shuafat
French Hill
Planned
extention
of
Maale
Edumim
EAST
JERUSALEM
ISRAEL
Old
WEST
City
JERUSALEM
Maale
Silouan
Edumim
Abu
Dis
East
Beit
Givat
Talpiot
Safafa
Hamatos
Sur
Sheikh
Bahir
Said
Gilo
Givat
Ha'Arba
Har
Ubadiya
Homa
Batfir
Har
Gilo
Beth Lehem
Zaatara
Al Khidr
Beit
Sahour
Khirbat
Al Makhrum
Daihaisha

N
W — E
S
0   2
scale in miles

——— Pre-1967 international border
----- City limit of Jerusalem before June 1967
——— City limit of Jerusalem post 1967
     Palestinian quarters, towns, villages
     Israeli settlements
····· Planned extensions of Israeli settlements

© 2004, Mark Stein Studios

MAP 10. THE GOLAN HEIGHTS.

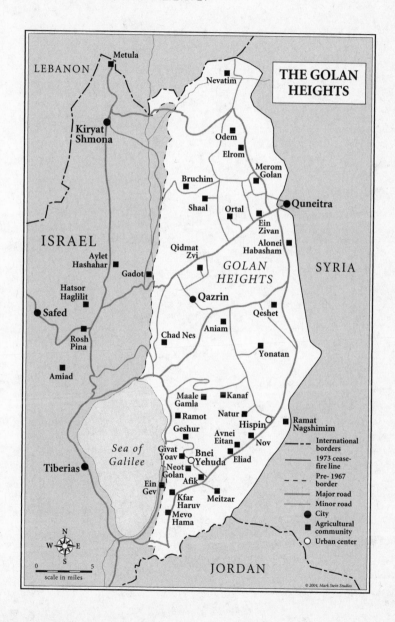

THE GOLAN HEIGHTS

LEBANON

Metula

Nevatim

Kiryat Shmona

Odem

Elrom

Merom Golan

Bruchim

Shaal

Ortal

Quneitra

Ein Zivan

ISRAEL

Aylet Hashahar

Gadot

Qidmat Zvi

Alonei Habasham

GOLAN HEIGHTS

SYRIA

Hatsor Haglilit

Safed

Qazrin

Qeshet

Chad Nes

Aniam

Rosh Pina

Yonatan

Amiad

Maale Gamla

Kanaf

Ramot

Natur

Hispin

Ramat Nagshimim

Geshur

Avnei Eitan

Nov

Sea of Galilee

Givat Yoav

Bnei Yehuda

Eliad

Neot Golan

Afik

Ein Gev

Kfar Haruv

Meitzar

Tiberias

Mevo Hama

International borders

1973 cease-fire line

Pre- 1967 border

Major road

Minor road

City

Agricultural community

Urban center

N
W   E
S

0   5
scale in miles

JORDAN

© 2004, Mark Stein Studios

DEFENDING ISRAEL

tarting around the turn of the twentieth century, when some of the earliest Zionist immigrants encountered opposition in their attempt to reclaim the Land of Israel, the Arab-Israeli conflict has now lasted for about a hundred years. Partly because the Middle East belonged to the Ottoman Empire, widely recognized as the Sick Man of Europe, and partly owing to the strategic and economic importance of the region, other powers—Britain, France, Germany, and, to a lesser extent, Austria-Hungary and Russia—were involved from the start. This was carried to the point where, in 1917–1918, Britain and France took over from Turkey, and from then on it was they who ruled the region; still, until 1948, the year that marked the creation of the State of Israel, the conflict remained localized. One reason for this was that both Jews and Arabs were far too weak and insignificant for their quarrels to disturb the peace of the world. Neither World War I nor World War II had its origins in the Middle East or was centered in it. Compared to those momentous events, whatever took place there was a sideshow.

In 1948–1973 the conflict escalated.[1] The periodic small-scale, mutual butchery that had characterized the Land of Israel during the 1920s and 1930s was followed by several major interstate wars, causing the country to be partitioned. In 1948 alone as many as 700,000 people were driven from their homes, whereas the 1967 War probably added another 250,000. Millions of others came to live under an occupation regime which, whatever the original intentions that led to it, became so prolonged as to appear permanent. Perhaps worst of all, a situation was repeatedly created whereby the most important global powers of the time, the U.S.A. and the U.S.S.R., confronted each other on behalf of their respective clients. Both made warlike noises, one sent its own uniformed personnel to assist the belligerents, and one went so far as to put its nuclear forces on alert; at other times, afraid that the flames might consume them both, they recoiled and tried to pour water on them.

Though the years since 1982 have not witnessed any large-scale military operations in the region, the conflict, particularly that part of it which involves Israel and the Palestinians, continues to fester. To be sure, the global crisis which was predicted by Samuel Huntington and reached its (temporary?) climax in the attacks on the Twin Towers and the Pentagon, and has pitted parts of the West against much of the Arab and Islamic world, is not just a by-product of the Palestinian-Israeli conflict. Still, that conflict does form an important element in the larger clash of civilizations.[2] Should it be resolved or at least de-escalated, then surely the latter will lose some of its sting.

For Israel itself, the writing is on the wall. In strictly military terms it has won every conventional war it fought against its larger neighbors, beating them time and again, inflicting more casualties than it took, and seizing additional territory until most of its adversaries more or less gave up the struggle and some concluded peace. To the extent that its victories resulted in the occupation of inhabited districts, however, they only caused it to become bogged down in an endless counterinsurgency campaign against the much weaker Palestinians; as Napoleon used to say of Spain, the conflict has turned into a running ulcer. Israel's morale is being undermined, its government is becoming less effective as lawlessness and corruption spread,[3] and civilian control over the military is weakening as several successive chiefs of staff have made direct appeals to public opinion.[4] Economically speaking the situation is equally bleak. Israel's GDP has begun to decline, causing its economic position to worsen both in comparison with some Arab countries and, a fortiori, other developed ones; this is the first time in twenty years that has happened. With unemployment standing at 12 percent, immigration has all but ceased.[5] Last, but not least, human losses are mounting. The number of dead and wounded is already larger than that suffered in the June 1967 War that led to the occupation in the first place. To put the matter into perspective, 2,800 people were killed in the events of 9-11, the largest act of terrorism ever. Compared to the size of the population, though, this is only one twelfth as many as Israel has lost to Palestinian terrorism since the current Uprising began in September 2000.

From time to time there is talk of a political solution called the Mitchell Plan, or the Tennet Plan, or the Road Map, or some such. Each time this happens a whole series of international luminaries show up in the Middle East. A few, primarily American ones, have real clout, but the majority do not. They shake hands all around, show themselves in front of as many cameras as possible, do their best to act as honest brokers in an all but hopeless situation, and, if the countries they represent are rich, promise some modest assistance as well. So far, with each plan, it has only been a matter of time before a spate of suicide bombings (by some Palestinian terrorist organization) and/or "targeted killings" (by the Israelis) makes sure they will fail. It is as if leaders on both sides are determined to kill enough people on the other to kindle the flames; talks lasting for months can be, and often are, derailed by an incident measured in seconds.

As a result, the best the present Israeli chief of staff, General Moshe Ya'alon, can promise, is that every Palestinian who commits a terrorist act will be punished either sooner or later[6]—a policy which, so far, has deterred few, if any, of them. Worse still, even if the Israel Defense Force (IDF) "wins" the conflict in some limited sense, hostilities will only be suspended until the other side recovers and feels strong enough to resume them. The very fact that the occupation continues will make sure that a fresh outbreak will take place every few years; meanwhile, since the rate of natural increase in the Territories is one of the highest in the world, time is working against Israel.

Most worrying of all is a deepening cleavage between Right and

Left that, if left to develop, may threaten Israeli society itself with disso-
lution. Already, the leaders of a country long known for its family-like
informality, move around in armored cars and under heavy escort. They
take all kinds of evasive action, directed as much against Jewish terrorists as against Arab ones. The security-related queues that form each
time a major figure such as Shimon Peres makes a public appearance
must be seen to be believed; no sooner did Ariel Sharon start talking of
returning some settlements in the summer of 2003 than threats on his
life multiplied many times. There is nothing insignificant about such
threats. In the words of a former minister of defense, Benjamin Ben
Eliezer, the next bullet through a prime minister's spine may kill not just
him but the country itself.

If Israel is lucky, then the end of the occupation will be brought
about by negotiation and agreement, and will be followed by the establishment of a cohesive Palestinian State willing to live in peace and capable of maintaining order within its borders. If, as in view of past
experience is perhaps more likely, it is not, then the withdrawal may
well have to be carried out unilaterally and the situation on the other
side be damned. This, after all, is what David Ben Gurion, himself an
outstanding authority on defense, said should be done immediately
after the victorious 1967 War; and what Prime Minister Ehud Barak,
overriding the objections of many of his advisers, did in Lebanon in
May 2000. Even if the most favorable scenario comes to pass, though, it
will be a long time before passions cool down and the Middle East becomes a place where war can be ruled out. Until that happens, Israel will
still have to look after its defense against the worst that the Palestinians,
the neighboring hostile Middle Eastern States (including, for good measure, such "under the horizon" enemies as Iran and Libya) or all of these
combined can do. The purpose of the present study is to ask what such
a defense might look like; and, indeed, whether it is possible at all.

In case the plan here outlined is not followed, then Israelis and
Palestinians may well be doomed to fight each other forever, with all

the attendant human, social, and economic consequences—not to mention the possible repercussions for the rest of the Middle East and, indeed, the world at large. If it is followed, though, then the struggle, though it may not come to an end, will almost certainly de-escalate. Israel will finally be relieved of a self-imposed burden under which it has been laboring for more years than the majority of its citizens can even remember. A notable feature of Israel has always been its formidable human energies. Cutting the chain that binds the fast, elegant, Israeli frigate off the leaking, barely seaworthy, Palestinian barge will enable it to focus those energies on a single task, i.e. developing the country. The period between 1993 and 2000, when the illusion of a coming peace caused the Israeli economy to double and for a time made the shekel into the strongest currency on earth, showed what could be done; and even that was just a foretaste of what the future may bring.

The outline of this brief book is as follows. Providing the background, chapter 1 examines the way Israel used to look after its security before it fought, and won, the 1967 War. Chapter 2 asks how the territorial gains made in that War affected Israel's security situation and how this spectacular victory paradoxically gave rise to the doctrine of "defensible borders." Chapter 3 looks at the grand strategic equation in the Middle East as it affects Israel's ability to defend itself, as well as the way in which a withdrawal from the Territories might affect that equation and that ability. Chapter 4 deals with defense against terrorism and guerrilla warfare, chapter 5 with defense against conventional war, and chapter 6 with defense against long-range air and surface-to-surface missile attack, including such as may carry weapons of mass destruction. Chapter 7 takes a brief look at some nonmilitary, nonstrategic, factors that affect Israel's defense. Finally, chapter 8 comprises my conclusions.

Since much of the present volume deals with the future rather than the past, and since the IDF is not in the habit of permitting outsiders to look at its future plans, my research has been limited almost entirely to published sources. I have grabbed them left and right, using whatever

I thought might shed light on the question at hand. Some of my arguments were unwittingly provided by right-wing extremists in Israel and abroad who, asked just what "defensible borders" meant and why Israel needed them, turned out to have either no answer at all or one that was based on the situation as it was over thirty years ago. Though I have not had the benefit of receiving any official assistance from the IDF,[7] I did have the opportunity to talk things over with some of its members. The most important of them was Colonel (ret.) Dr. Shmuel Gordon. Gordon is a one-time commander of a squadron of F-16s, a military consultant, and a former student of mine; having spent years studying the subject, he probably knows more about the Revolution in Military Affairs (RMA) than any other Israeli does. Of the rest, some agreed with what I had to say, others not. To all of them, I am grateful.

Before ending this introduction, I want to thank the Axel and Margaret Axson Johnson Foundation, Stockholm, for providing financial aid, without which the writing of this book would have been impossible. Thanks are also due—once again—to Zeev Elron and Dvora Lewy. The former has gone over the manuscript with his usual meticulous eye, telling me how wrong I was and correcting for errors; if there are any left, it is my fault rather than his. The latter has been my partner in life during the last twenty years. Normally her contribution to my work consists of everything that only a good marriage can provide, which is very much indeed. This time, though, she gave me still more; namely, the very idea of putting the question at hand and trying to answer it. Since the idea underlying this study was originally hers, and since, in my view, our common future and that of our children depends on its conclusions being adopted, it is only fit that I put my gratitude to her on record.

Considering the alleged "indefensibility" of Israel's pre-1967 borders, how *did* the State defend itself during the first nineteen years of its existence when it was much weaker than it is today? To answer this question, let us start by looking at some maps published at the time. Except on the west, where it borders the Mediterranean, Israel was surrounded by enemies on all sides. So long were its land frontiers, and so small the territory they enclosed, that there was hardly any spot more than thirty miles from the nearest hostile border. From the Jordanian-held town of Kalkilya to the shore the distance was only ten miles; a drawing by Israel's best-known cartoonist took advantage of the twists and turns in the border to present it in the form of an angry snake, ready to strike. As legend had it, tourists journeying from Haifa to Tel Aviv and having a sausage in their possession were advised to hold it from north to south to prevent the Arabs from slicing off a part when they passed the narrowest point. Seriously, an armored force stationed in the foothills of the West Bank and seeking to reach the coast would have been able to do so in less than an hour, effectively cutting the country in half.

Then as now, Israel's heartland was greater Tel Aviv, which held about one quarter of the entire population and also comprised the economic heartland. Yet it was threatened by Egyptian troops stationed in the Gaza Strip, perhaps forty miles to the south, as well as Jordanian ones standing fewer than twenty miles to the east. During the 1967 War its northern neighborhoods came under the latter's artillery fire, albeit most of the shells fell harmlessly into the sea. Haifa, the main and, until the 1960s, only Mediterranean port and an important industrial center, was only about twenty-five miles from the Jordanian border and at about an equal distance from the Lebanese one. The position of the port of Eilat, which served as Israel's only artery to south and east Asia (violating the 1949 Armistice Agreements, the Egyptians did not permit Israeli shipping, or even foreign ships carrying loads destined for Israel, to pass the Suez Canal) was even more difficult. It was, and still is, the world's only city that is located where the borders of four countries (Israel, Egypt, Jordan, and Saudi Arabia) meet. To cut it off, all the Egyptians had to do was move their forces some ten miles to the east.

Perhaps worst of all was the position of the capital, West Jerusalem. Reflecting the outcome of the 1948 War, it was located at the apex of a triangle jutting into Jordanian territory and surrounded on three sides. The highest point of all, Mount Nebi Samuel, was also in Jordanian hands. In 1948 it had served to rain down artillery shells on the city; several Israeli attempts to capture it had failed. Of the roads leading into the capital only one was really suitable for modern traffic, and that one ran so close to the border that smugglers from both sides sometimes met right besides it. The railroad that linked the city to Tel Aviv, indeed, *was* the border; occasionally it was blocked as Arab kids from neighboring villages put stones on the tracks. During the 1948 War both those arteries had been closed for a period of about three months, which led to the loss of the old Jewish quarter—it was taken by the Jordanians on 28 May—and brought the city close to starvation. Both in the center, where the Jordanians overlooked the coastal plain, and in the north of the country, where the Syrians occupied the dominating Golan Heights and used them as a base for harassing the Israeli settlements in the Jordan Valley, it was Israel's enemies who occupied the high ground. They thus enjoyed all the advantages that doing so entails. When Israeli Foreign Minister Abba Eban once spoke of "Auschwitz borders," he had a point, though he was no military expert and he later modified that statement.

And yet, the difficulties were not insuperable. In part, this was because the borders, though they were completely without logic and though they cut right across countless streams, valleys, and transportation arteries, turned out not to constitute a serious obstacle to the country's development. The latter proceeded as if those borders, and with them the hostile states on the other sides, did not exist; proof, if proof were needed, that it is primarily human ingenuity and not geography that makes a society tick.[1] Nor were the military problems that these borders created nearly as bad as they seemed at first sight. To quote a wise saying by Moshe Dayan, the road from Tel Aviv to Damascus was no longer than the one which led from Damascus to Tel Aviv; in fact, even taking the pre-1967 border as one's starting point, it was considerably shorter. Take the Gaza Strip. To anyone familiar with the map the Strip, some twenty-five miles long and less than seven miles wide in most places, looks like a finger pointing straight at Tel Aviv. During the 1948 War it was occupied by the Egyptian Army, which, having overrun the few Jewish settlements in the area, turned it into a forward base and used it to advance to within twenty-five or so miles of that city. In fact, however, since there are no topographical obstacles of any kind, the finger is hopelessly exposed to an invasion from two directions. It is also narrow enough so that its entire length can be brought under artillery bombardment both from the land and the sea.

Above all, the Strip hinges on Rafa, the southern town that marks the border between it and the Sinai, and the site of a T-junction where the coastal road meets one that runs to the southeast. Already, in late 1948, a small Israeli infantry unit, launching a bayonet charge, had occupied a hill overlooking the town; the only reason why it could not press home its advantage was because it possessed no heavy weapons to confront the Egyptians. Although, by 1956, the town and its surroundings had been heavily fortified, it still took an Israeli armored division, ineffectively assisted by gunfire from a French destroyer, just one night's hard fighting to break through the Egytian positions. In 1967 the same operation was carried out in broad daylight on the first day of the Six Days' War and only took a few hours to accomplish; to the extent that the Egyptians were able to put up any resistance it was mainly symbolic. By that time, so hopeless had any attempt to defend the Strip become that, had it been up to Dayan, it would not have been attacked at all but left to fall of itself as Israeli forces, bypassing it to the southwest, raced towards the Suez Canal. In the event, what all three campaigns really showed was how easy it was to cut the Strip from the rest of the Sinai Peninsula, causing any forces unfortunate enough to be stationed in it to be trapped.

Appearances to the contrary, the situation in the West Bank was similar. It is true that Jordanian control over that part of the country provided them with excellent starting positions from which to cut off Jerusalem, dominate and harass the coastal plain, and invade Israel from the east. It is equally true, though, that the border between Jordan and Israel was no longer than the one between Israel and Jordan. Throughout the period from 1949 to 1967, but particularly in 1953–5, it was the Israeli Army that demonstrated its power by launching countless raids into the West Bank. The blood toll, both military and civilian, ran into many hundreds, perhaps more. Except for two very small moves during the 1967 War itself, though, not once in all that period did a single Jordanian soldier penetrate a single inch into Israeli territory proper; and even those thrusts were repelled without any difficulty within a few hours.

Partly because they were afraid of what the Israelis might do to them, partly because they often had Syria, Egypt and (after 1958), Ba'athist Iraq to cope with as well, most of the time the Jordanians did what they could to ensure that the border should remain peaceful. In this they were not always successful, as happened, for example, in November 1966, when infiltrators crossed into Israel and blew up a patrol vehicle, inflicting casualties. Upon being informed of the incident King Hussein sent a note to apologize, promising to punish the perpetrators, but before it could be delivered the Israelis retaliated by raiding the village of Samua, near Hebron, and all but demolished it.[2] As a Jordanian

Army unit came to the rescue it was ambushed, and over seventy of its troops were killed or wounded. Four 1950s-vintage Jordanian fighter aircraft appeared overhead and tried to interfere in the battle, but were chased away by Israeli Mirages. No wonder that, writing their after-action report, the Israelis spoke of "poor little Jordan" and concluded they would have no difficulty overrunning the entire West Bank in short order.[3] A mere seven months later they did exactly that. Even as their main striking forces battled the Egyptians, they took less than three days to accomplish the feat. Indeed, so easy was the operation that, as in the case of the Gaza Strip, large parts of it were carried out by the Officers Commanding, Northern and Central Fronts, on their own initiative and without waiting for orders from Moshe Dayan. He himself would have been content by occupying only a fairly narrow strip along the border, making it harder for the Jordanians to target some Israeli assets but leaving the most important cities in their hands, or so he later claimed in his memoirs.[4]

Jordanian military weakness apart, one reason why the Bank was so hard to defend was because, in the entire territory, there was (and is) just one road linking the southern bulge to the northern one. Connecting Hebron with Bethlehem, Ramallah, Nablus, and Jenin, for most of its length it ran roughly along the watershed, staying perhaps fifteen to twenty miles away from the nearest Israeli border and thus providing reasonable security against attack, except from the air. However, the section that led northward from Bethlehem to Ramallah had to cross East Jerusalem, as it still does. It passed within a few hundred yards of that border; a winding, twisting affair, only one lane wide and more suitable for the occasional vehicle than for a steady flow of modern traffic. Just as the main road from Tel Aviv to Jerusalem was within striking range of the Jordanians, so the Israelis could have cut the Bank in half within five minutes of the order being given. This, of course, is one reason why the Palestinians have always insisted on having East Jerusalem as their capital and will not give up on it. Even disregarding its symbolic importance, without it all they can have is not a state but two separate cantons linked, if they can be linked at all, by a waist as narrow as that of an ant.

While building activities that have taken place since then make it hard to reconstruct the layout of the terrain, it is not impossible that the Israelis could have cut the West Bank in two without engaging in any ground movements at all. To adduce just one example of how it could have been done, take the northwestern corner of the Old City between the Ottoman-built wall on the one hand and the great Hostel of Notre Dame which, at that time, was in ruins. Running across the street between the hostel and the city wall there was another wall that separated the Israeli side from the Jordanian. From the place where Israel ended, as people used to say, the distance to the above-mentioned road was only about three-quarters of a mile, looking downhill. All that was needed was to break down the wall that marked the border, bring up two heavy self-propelled artillery pieces, and open fire over open sights. These considerations explain why, at the time of the 1949 Armistice Agreements, the Jordanians insisted that West Jerusalem be kept free of heavy weapons and, after much bargaining, got their way. Once the Agreements were broken, the rest followed almost automatically; to this day, whoever controls Jerusalem holds the key to the entire area.

Penetrating into enemy territory, salients have their uses in maneuver warfare. On the other hand, they are exposed to such warfare; by definition, anything that can serve as a forward base can also be cut off. Then as now, the Bank formed a salient—or, in view of what has just been said, two almost entirely separate salients—into Israeli territory that surrounded it on three sides. A pincer movement coming from the south was ruled out by the terrain west of the Dead Sea, where sheer mountains descend directly to the shore and where there was no road. On the other hand, Israeli forces coming from the north (the Beth Shean Valley) would enjoy more room for maneuver and find it almost as easy to pinch off the West Bank as it was for Jordanian ones to slice

Israel in half. To put it in a different way, as long as Israel's own armed forces remained intact and capable of maneuvering, for an opponent to send his army from the eastern Jordanian plateau across the Jordan River into the West Bank simply meant inserting it into a killing ground. The more so because the terrain, which rises from 1,200 feet under the sea to 2,200 feet above it, constitutes a formidable obstacle.

These considerations may explain why, historically speaking, most of those who invaded the Land of Israel did so by using the road that ran along the Mediterranean Coast. Either they proceeded from the north (by way of what is now Lebanon) or the south (coming from Egypt). For those coming from Syria, another possibility was to cross the Jordan River, either north or immediately south of the Sea of Galilee, and then head west towards the Valley of Esdraelon; that, for example, was the route Saladin, on his way to the Battle of Hattin, took in 1187. By contrast, few if any armies tried to cross the Jordan River further south, between the Sea of Galilee and the Dead Sea. Among the very few exceptions was the Arab Legion in 1948; that, however, was only possible because the British permitted it (at the time, the Legion formed part of the Imperial Forces and was commanded by British officers). Another reason was because there was no opposition. The entire area did not contain a single Jewish settlement that could have served as a point d'appui for organizing a defense. Nor were any Jewish armed forces stationed there; nor did the Jews have long-range weapons such as attack aircraft capable of commanding it from afar. Before 1948, the last time anybody tried to invade the Land of Israel from the direction of the desert was over 3,000 years ago, when Joshua led his tribesmen to Jericho. Unlike Joshua, the commanders of the Jordanian Army did not have magic trumpets to bring down walls. Perfectly aware that the West Bank constituted a trap, during most of the period 1948–1967 they were careful to keep their main forces stationed well east of the River.

One person who was well aware of the plus and minuses of the geo-strategic situation was the IDF's real founder and its second Chief of Staff, Major General Yigael Yadin. A protege of Ben Gurion, during the 1948 War Yadin had been Chief of Operations. He spent much of it moving his forces, now here, now there, in a desperate attempt to head off threats coming from various directions. Later he and his subordinates, including a certain twenty-nine-year colonel named Yitzhak Rabin who was head of the Operations Department, started working on a doctrine that would offset the country's weaknesses while utilizing its assets to the maximum possible effect.[5] The doctrine's most important pillar was deterrence, a product of Israel's demonstrated ability and willingness to cut off the hand that was raised against it, as the saying went. Should deterrence fail and war come about, then Israel was to place its trust in good intelligence that would provide it with early warning of a coming attack. Early warning in turn would permit rapid mobilization of all available resources and their concentration at the most endangered spots—which, interestingly, did not include the Israeli-Jordanian border. Critical to the entire exercise was a centralized, yet highly flexible, command system. This was something that Israel possessed, whereas its Arab enemies, eternally divided by their internal squabbles, did not.

Whereas the early plans hesitated between the defensive and the offensive, from at least July 1951 on the emphasis was clearly on the latter. First the strongest enemy, Egypt, then the rest, would be crushed, and the war "carried into the enemy's territory," as the official phraseology went. At a minimum, the IDF was to reach as far as the River Litani in Lebanon, the Damascus-Irbid-Amman-Aqaba line in Jordan, and El Arish in Egypt.[6] Some plans, particularly those drawn up by a young Lieutenant Colonel Yuval Neeman (the subsequently world-famous nuclear scientist) were much more ambitious still. If there existed any doubts concerning Israel's ability to smash its enemies when the opportunity presented itself, the files of the General Staff are the wrong place to look for them; in 1954 the dovish Moshe Sharet, who in his capacity as prime minister was permitted to peep at them, called them "monstrous."

Preparing for the strike, Israel was to build up powerful fighting forces consisting mainly of squadrons of attack aircraft and armored brigades. The former would protect the country's skies, defeat the enemy's air force, achieve air superiority, and aid the ground forces by interdicting the enemy and flying close support missions. The latter would strike hard and fast, driving spearheads into vulnerable parts of the enemy array, cutting his forces into penny packets and smashing them.

Partly because Israel was such a poor country, partly because several Western countries refused to provide it with arms, some of the hardware needed to implement the doctrine proved hard to obtain so the plans it was designed to serve remained on paper. Even in 1956 some of the weapons were still missing, but this did not prevent the doctrine from being tested for the first time. The political gains of the Suez campaign were mediocre at best, but militarily it was a crushing success. The Israelis' first move was to concentrate their best troops—the 202nd Paratroop Brigade, commanded by none other than Ariel Sharon—on the Jordanian border south of the Dead Sea by way of a feint. Next they turned west and, storming into the Sinai by air and by land, overran it in a campaign that lasted all of six days. At a cost of only 170 dead, the Egyptian Army with its three divisions was smashed; albeit some of the work was done by Israel's French and British allies, who joined the campaign seventy-two hours after its start. Both in Israel and abroad, the conclusion was that not even the strongest Arab army was a match for the Israeli one. As one battalion commander, a future chief of staff, wrote, fighting the Egyptians was like playing chess against an opponent who, for every two moves of one's own, was only allowed to make one.[7]

By 1967, the doctrine had become well established and the means for implementing it had also become available. When war came in that year, Israel's armed forces were to those of its combined enemies as one to two and a half.[8] Partly for financial reasons, partly because some Western countries still refused to provide Israel with military hardware, by international standards much of its arsenal was out of date. In many ways, the forces that inflicted a crushing defeat on those of Egypt, Syria, and Jordan looked as if they had come straight out of World War II. This was particularly true of the ground forces and the navy. The former still drove Sherman tanks and M-3 half-tracks, though more modern fighting vehicles such as the M-48 Patton tank were also being introduced. The navy did not even own a radar station of its own, having to rely on the air force in this respect. What it did own was an incredible assortment of secondhand, decades-old, destroyers, torpedo boats, submarines, and landing craft; so bad was the situation that there was even some talk of abolishing it altogether and letting the air force do its work. By contrast, from the mid-1950s on the principal Arab countries received their weapons mainly from the Soviet Union, and many of them were among the most modern that country possessed.

Israel's numerical inferiority was to some extent offset by the internal lines on which it operated, permitting it to shift units rapidly from one front to another. Particularly in the air, this helps explain how they were able to smash the combined air forces in just one day; on the ground, too, the IDF's offensive potential was augmented by approximately 25 to 30 percent. In 1967 some units of paratroopers intended for the Sinai ended up fighting as infantry on the Jordanian front, where they were responsible for capturing East Jerusalem. Entire brigades fought first the Jordanians and then, having helped finish off that opponent, the Syrians; at least one managed to drive all the way from the Sinai to the Golan Heights and saw action on both fronts. By contrast, geography, including above all the barrier formed by the Red Sea, prevented the main Arab belligerents from sending more than token forces to each other's aid. To say nothing of the fact that, when the time came and the Egyptian and Jordanian armies were trounced by the IDF, the Syrians chose to stand by with their arms folded. As so often they used their artillery to shell the Israeli settlements in the Jordan Valley; they did not, however, make a serious offensive move.

Meanwhile, the inferiority of many of Israel's weapons was offset by its superior military-industrial infrastructure. Originating in pre-state days, since 1948 it has undergone steady development. By the 1960s, though it was still very modest by world standards, it enabled some old weapons to be upgraded; others, including the critically important Durendal runaway-busting bomb,[9] were developed from scratch. In addition there were superior maintenance and repair facilities, a superior command and control mechanism, and superior training. All this was made possible by a much better educated population; giving the IDF a qualitative edge subsequent commentators estimated at between 1.5 to 1 (vis-à-vis the Jordanians) to 3.5 to 1 (vis-à-vis the Palestinians).[10] Last but not least, Israel, unlike its enemies, was—and, so far, has remained— a democracy, more or less. Not having to fear a military coup or hold some of its forces in reserve to watch its own citizens, it could and did throw in everything it had.

As the events of 1967 showed, the level where Israel found itself at the greatest disadvantage was not the tactical and operational but the strategic and grand strategic. Israel's population was small—less than 2.5 million Jews confronted about 40 million Arabs—and it did not have strategic depth. Hence, the risk it took by going to war was much greater. As Ben Gurion was fond of saying, the first battle lost might well be the last;[11] one of those who liked to repeat his words was Ariel Sharon. Since Israel depended on mobilization, having to wage war on any scale was certain to disrupt its society and its economy. In other words, Israel could only sustain the fight for a limited time, forcing it to go on the offensive whether it wanted to or not. Yet at the same time there were limits to what even the most successful offensive could achieve; translating military victory into political achievement was difficult if not impossible.

In part, this was because of the far larger populations and territories that its enemies commanded. In part, it was because those enemies were to some extent protected against total defeat by their Superpower patrons, i.e. the U.S.S.R. in the case of Egypt and Syria and the U.S. in the case of Jordan. In 1973, as in 1967 and 1956, each time it looked as if Israel was about to inflict a crushing blow on its enemies the Security Council, reflecting the wishes of the Great Powers, would meet and impose a cease-fire. As early as January 1949 Israeli forces advancing into the Sinai had been halted by a British ultimatum; but for it, the Egyptian forces in the Gaza Strip would have been surrounded and forced to surrender. The Arab leaders were well aware of these facts. Unlike Israel, they never had to contemplate the prospect of annihilation; their societies, if not necessarily their armies, would always live to fight another day. This enabled them to go to war more easily, sustain the fight longer, and risk less by doing so.

Still, those Arab advantages were to a large extent offset by other factors. The first was the exceptionally high motivation that permeated both Israeli society and its army. In part, that motivation reflected the Jews' recent history in the form of the Holocaust, when one third of all Jews had been killed, giving rise to the feeling of "never again." In part, it was a direct result of the difficult strategic situation itself; expressing itself in the famous words, *en brera* ("no choice"). The second factor was the nuclear option. The decision to develop nuclear weapons seems to have been made by Ben Gurion in the mid-1950s.[12] As part of the deal that antedated the launching of the 1956 Suez Campaign, France provided Israel with a reactor and a plutonium-separation plant, as well as hundreds of technicians who worked on the project until relations between the two countries started deteriorating during the early 1960s.[13] To it, the Arab countries had absolutely no answer. Of these factors, the first played a cardinal role in making possible Israel's smashing victory in the 1967 War. The second made fairly certain that, even if the first had not been present or had proved insufficient to bring about victory, the Jewish State would have survived, if the worst came to the worst.

To sum up, and as events demonstrated in the most spectacular way possible, defending Israel within the pre-1967 borders was a very difficult, but far from insoluble, task. In part, this was because geography is like time, creating both difficulties and opportunities. On balance it works in favor of the side that makes the best use of it; the more so because, as I have shown, the situation was not nearly as bad as appeared to be the case at first sight, and much better than anyone looking back might think. In part it was because, as has been said, there is nothing like a death sentence to focus the mind; and Israel before 1967 was convinced, not without some reason, that it was facing a death sentence every day. In part it was because Israel, though its resources were smaller than those of its enemies, also possessed certain advantages that enabled it to better utilize those resources which it did have. Confident in their overall superiority and tending to despise the Jews, the Arab leaders might bluster about their determination never to recognize the Zionist Entity (whose name many of them even refused to pronounce) and to destroy it at the first opportunity. However, when the call for action came it was not they but Israel and its army who were like a coiled spring, ready for release. To make them deliver a knockout blow, all that was necessary was to pull the trigger.

G iven that the June 1967 War provided a spectacular demonstration of Israel's ability to defeat its enemies, how on earth did its
leaders convince themselves that the country's security could not be
guaranteed unless the Territories it had just occupied were retained? To
answer that question, Hebrew readers can turn to a fascinating study
that first saw the light of print in 1996. Its author, Dr. Reuven Pedatzur,
lectures in political science at Tel Aviv University while also serving as a
defense correspondent for *Haaretz*, one of Israel's leading newspapers.
A former fighter pilot in the Israel Air Force, he is especially known for
his opposition to the Arrow antiballistic defense system which he has
long opposed and still opposes.[1] To write his book he was given access
to classified cabinet records pertaining to the period between 1967 and
1970, which form his principal source and which he was the first to
publish.

The title of Pedatzur's book, *The Triumph of Embarrassment,*
speaks for itself. The present borders of the Land of Israel—including
both Israel and any eventual Palestinian State—were determined in
1920–1922 by a British committee headed by Winston Churchill, who
at that time was serving as Colonial Secretary. Not all Zionists accepted this decision, and some right-wingers among them claimed
much wider borders. They even had a hymn, "The Jordan Has Two
Banks, and Both of Them Are Ours," which they later passed to the ancestor of the present Likud Party; as late as 1967 their voice was still
occasionally heard. However, even they did not do so because they
considered the country's borders "indefensible." Instead they based
their aspirations—which very few people at the time took seriously—

on ideological and theological grounds.[2] This, after all, was the country God had promised His People, or so some of those who read the Bible claimed. Its present-day Arab-speaking population was where it was merely due to some historical accident which would be rectified by vigorous action on Israel's part. Some thought of expelling them; others, of converting them (back to, as they alleged) to Judaism as if Mohammed and 1,300 years of history had never existed.

More interesting than these fantasies, which in any case were only the province of a very small minority and which tended to lose their importance as time went on, is the fact that the concept of "defensible borders" was not even part of the IDF's own vocabulary. Anyone who will look for it in the military literature of the time will do so in vain. Instead, Israel's commanders based their thought on the 1948 War and, especially, their 1956 triumph over the Egyptians, in which, from then chief of staff Dayan down, they had gained their spurs. When the 1967 crisis broke they felt certain of their ability to win a "decisive, quick and elegant" victory, as one of their number, General Haim Bar Lev, put it, and pressed the government to start the war as soon as possible.

While the General Staff met the occasion by putting on a show of confidence, the popular mood had bordered on panic. Food was hoarded and Tel Aviv parks were ritually consecrated to serve as cemeteries capable of holding as many as 20,000 people; this panic, in turn, reflected on the country's civilian leaders. Some worried about the fact that, contrary to the situation in 1956, no Great Power had openly arrayed itself on Israel's side. Others were elderly men and women who carried terrible memories from the Holocaust and, perhaps understandably, tended to think in apocalyptic terms. In and outside Israel at the time it was fashionable to compare Nasser with Hitler; both hated Jews, and both would only have their appetites whetted by attempts to appease them.[3] The prevailing image was of hordes of Arab savages, knives held between their teeth, eagerly preparing to slaughter the Jews to the last man, woman, and child. Such scenes had, in fact, taken place during the

Arab Revolts of 1929 and 1936–1939, as well as during the 1948 War itself. Nor, to anybody who recalls the dancing crowds in the Arab capitals, was the image altogether without foundation. All this explains why, once the War had been won, those leaders were determined never to allow Israel's previous situation to return or to withdraw to the old borders. This view was reinforced by a surge of popular Messianic feeling that some of them shared and which few could entirely ignore. To many Israelis, and not just orthodox ones, it seemed as if God Himself had been fighting on their side and pointing the way.

As already mentioned, the one important exception was David Ben Gurion. Unlike some of the younger generation, who had grown up in the country itself and knew remarkably little about what went on outside it, Ben Gurion prided himself on his wide-ranging, humanist education and had always been sensitive to the problems of modern nationalism. In October 1948 he had refused his subordinates' requests that they be allowed to conquer the West Bank—which they could have done easily enough—precisely because he did not want any more Arabs inside Israel's borders.[4] Instead he ordered them to wrest the Negev Desert from the Egyptian Army, which had invaded it; being all but empty of people, he thought the region could be made to blossom with the aid of modern science. During the years that followed some of his subordinates, the most senior of whom was Dayan, continued to toy with the idea of exploiting some border incident in order to "destabilize" Jordan, overthrow its Hashemite rulers, and complete the job. He, however, held them back, insisting that his decision had been right all along and that Israel had nothing to gain from such an operation. Security was the result of wider factors including immigration, education, and general progress; the idea that new borders would improve it, he thought, was "a delusion."[5]

When the June 1967 crisis broke, Ben Gurion, then eighty years old, had been out of power for four years. He spent most of that time heaping abuse upon his successor, Levi Eshkol, whom he accused of every possible sin including, above all, some mysterious "security-related fail-ure." Apparently what he had in mind was Eshkol's agreement to permit the Americans to inspect the nuclear reactor Israel was constructing at Dimona. Visiting him two weeks before the War broke out, Chief of Staff Yitzhak Rabin thought the former prime minister was out of touch. His ideas of world events had something quaint about them, nor did he re-alize how strong the IDF had become;[6] he was terrified of the coming war and did what little he could to dissuade his former protege, Dayan, from launching it. As things turned out, the outcome of the War seemed to prove that his claims were unfounded. This caused both the public and governing circles to see him as a cantankerous old man, and his de-mand that Israel should return "everything except Jerusalem"—whose century-old walls, incidentally, he wanted to demolish—was met with smiles of disdain.

With the exception of Ben Gurion, a consensus that the old borders were "insecure" and could not be defended was quick to emerge. Yet just what borders *could* be defended and *were* secure was much less clear; the more so because, seen from a purely military point of view without con-sidering the political situation, the question was almost meaningless. In time this led to various plans, including at least one American map pre-pared by the Joint Chiefs of Staff and submitted to President Johnson. On that map, the northeastern Sinai, the Straits of Tiran and a corridor leading to it, the Gaza Strip, and parts of the West Bank and the Golan Heights were marked in black as being "vital" for defense. What those who ordered the map and prepared it were hoping to achieve is not clear, nor do we know whether it ever reached Johnson's eyes. Even if it did, apparently it was seen as more likely to obstruct negotiations than to help them forward. Accordingly it was relegated *ad acta,* from whence it was dug up only recently, a historical relic without any signif-icance.[7]

At the time, Israel's leading expert in the field was Minister of De-fense Moshe Dayan. In May 1948 Dayan had spent a day or two around

Dgania fighting the Syrians, forming a low opinion of them and claiming that, like birds, they could be scattered by a few bangs.[8] Later in the War of Independence he served as governor of Jerusalem, a position from which he negotiated with the Jordanians, helping Israel wrest additional slices of territory from them; in 1956, now serving as chief of staff, he led his forces to victory against the Egyptians. No wonder he considered the most important areas to be the Gaza Strip, the Straits of Tiran, and the north-south watershed running through the mountains of Judea and Samaria. The importance of preventing the first of these areas from ever again serving as an Egyptian base does not need to be pointed out. Concerning the second he once said, famously, that he preferred the Straits without peace to peace without the Straits; not without reason, since both the 1956 and the 1967 Wars had originated partly in Egypt's refusal to let Israeli shipping pass through them. The third area he considered indispensable for obtaining early warning of, and defending against, any offensive across the River Jordan. To ensure it did not elude Israel's grasp, he suggested that the government build five military bases. Each was to be surrounded by "fists" of Jewish settlements; in all, he planned to confiscate 25,000 acres of land for that purpose. On the other hand, he laid little store on the Golan Heights, claiming that Syria was "not a threat" to Israel. Had it depended on him, they might not have been occupied in the first place.[9]

Dayan's principal adversary in the cabinet was Minister of Labor—later, he also became Deputy Prime Minister—Yigal Allon. Two years younger than Dayan, the two first met in the late 1930s and had been rivals ever since. In May 1941 both of them participated in the British invasion of Syria, where they served as guides and where Dayan lost an eye. The injury caused Dayan's career to slow down, the more so because he had already spent eighteen months in a British prison for carrying arms. Meanwhile, that of Allon took off. It culminated in his appointment, at the ripe old age of twenty-eight as commander of PAL-MACH, the pre-state striking force that later provided many of the

Israeli Army's commanders; from which, however, he and his comrades were careful to exclude Dayan, who already possessed the reputation of a lone wolf. During the 1948 War he far outranked Dayan, acting as Israel's outstanding field commander. Together with Rabin, who served as his chief of staff, he led offensives in every part of the country, crowning his achievement by routing the Egyptian Army, which he chased into the Sinai. Had it depended on him, he would have continued the war until the last Jordanian soldier, too, had been driven across the Jordan River.

In late 1949, Allon was dismissed from the army by Ben Gurion, who disliked his left-wing politics. He was able to keep in touch with military matters by way of his former subordinates, among whom there were at least four future chiefs of staff as well as countless other generals. Later he also wrote a book on Israel's defense,[10] thus consolidating his reputation as a defense expert; the very term "defensible borders" seems to have originated with him. Unlike Dayan, who wanted to retain the north-south watershed above all, Allon insisted that the most important requirement was to separate the West Bank from the Arab countries further to the east. Accordingly, the really vital areas were the Jordan Valley and a corridor leading to it from Jerusalem. This idea had the added advantage that, whereas the watershed was heavily populated, the areas in question consisted of desert and were practically empty. Even the thousands of refugees from the 1948 War who had lived in it before June 1967 were gone, partly because the Israelis had driven them out, and partly out of their own free will; as the British Ambassador to Israel put it, "maximum security, minimum Arabs."[11]

Allon, though, also had another card up his sleeve. In the face of numerous incidents taking place along the Israeli-Syrian border before 1967, Dayan at one point had suggested that some of the Jordan Valley settlements might be uprooted and rebuilt further to the west. According to an interview that was only published many years after his death, he even came to see the occupation of the Golan as perhaps the worst error he ever made. He freely admitted that the Syrians were "sons of bitches"; that in itself, however, was "no reason for screwing them."[12] Being himself a member of Ginossar, a kibbutz located on the western shore of the Sea of Galilee, Allon could not disagree more. Not only did he consider the idea of moving settlements blasphemous—that was true of most Israelis—but he could not turn a deaf ear to the pleas of his neighbors who lived in that area and whose lives had long been made hell by Syrian artillery bombardments. Throughout the War he did what he could to press the Government to attack the Syrians, organizing delegations of fellow-kibbutzniks who came to Jerusalem "straight from the battlefield," as they said. No sooner had the War ended than, with his encouragement, but without any formal government authorization, the first Israeli settlers arrived on the Golan Heights and started establishing offshoots of their native kibbutzim. There and in other parts of the Territories, the more settlements that were built the more important it became to defend them and the less conceivable a withdrawal. Thus it was the tail that came to wag the dog.[13]

In the event, neither Eshkol nor his successor, Ms. Golda Meir, ever ruled on the matter. In large part it was the Arabs' fault. Meeting at the Khartoum Summit at the end of July, their heads of state famously rejected the possibility of negotiation, recognition, and peace; this was a resolution, incidentally, which has not been formally recalled to the present day and which gave Israel the best possible excuse to evade the issue. Partly it was because Israeli military strength was so superior that the matter did not appear urgent; as Dayan once put it, Israel could afford to wait for the Arabs to call. At that time and for many years after 1967 the forces needed to keep down the Territories were negligible, consisting of just a few battalions; nor was Israel, supported by the U.S., susceptible to the kind of international pressure that had forced it to evacuate the Sinai back in 1957. Within the Israeli cabinet, opinions were divided. Early position papers, submitted by experts even as the War was still going on, suggested that Sinai and the Golan Heights—but not the West Bank, where ideology counted for much more—should be evacuated in return for peace.[14] Eshkol himself went on record as saying that, "of course we do not want a centimeter of Syrian territory."[15] Others held a different view, claiming that the land in question had not been "conquered" but "liberated" and insisting that every inch of it be retained forever.

Though both Eshkol and Meir were necessarily involved with defense matters, neither was, or pretended to be, a military expert. The former was the quintessential civilian who, in a country where practically every youth did some form of military service, had never handled a rifle or spent a day in uniform. Until he was forced to give up the defense portfolio on the eve of the War he had relied on Chief of Staff Rabin for advice, treating him as a kind of military oracle; now that he no longer held it, his self-confidence suffered. The latter, as she herself admitted, did not even know what a division is[16]—a strange confession to come from the leader of a country that has always lived by its sword, and never more so than precisely at the time when she held office.

In the course of their careers, both Eshkol and Meir had had close encounters with Dayan. As leader of the "Young Generation" of Ben Gurion's MAPAI (the ancestor of today's Labor Party) in the late 1950s, Dayan tried to unseat them and take their places. That struggle proved premature and ended in 1964 when he resigned from the cabinet. Still, they had good reason to dislike him and fear him. No man was better at weaving intrigues or turning people against each other; praising them to their face only to stab them in the back. Though the June 1967 War had made Dayan into a popular idol and his position as minister of defense too strong to be assailed, he could still be outflanked. To that end Eshkol, and even more so Meir, relied on Allon, who was a much more gentlemanly character. They also brought in another pre-state military commander, left-wing politician, and cabinet member by the name of Israel Galili; realizing full well that anything the minister of defense might propose would immediately be contradicted by the other two.

Ms. Meir's desire to rein in Dayan may also explain why, when the time came to select a new chief of staff in 1971, she insisted on appointing General David Elazar against the express wishes of her most important colleague.

While two prime ministers preferred to divide instead of rule, events acquired their own momentum. More and more settlements were built—not just on the Golan Heights but, increasingly, in the West Bank and the Sinai as well. Some settlements were established without any authorization from above, the work of Israeli groups and individuals who had suddenly discovered their religious mission in life as well as an inexplicable desire to live amidst the very Arabs whom they professed to dislike and despise. Most, however, found at least one cabinet minister prepared to support them, either before or after the fact. This sometimes made for strange bedfellows. For example, the secular-minded socialist, Yigal Allon, assisted the ultra-religious fanatics who could think of no better place to live than in the middle of the ancient city of Hebron with its tens of thousands of Palestinian inhabitants. Later, the very first settlement in Samaria received the blessing of Shimon Peres. This was many years before he acquired his reputation as a leading dove; apparently his intention was to use it as a battering ram to reinforce his own authority against that of his old rival, Yitzhak Rabin.

While these intrigues were being woven, other settlements were less controversial and were set up with full government authorization and funding. This was particularly true of those in the Jordan Valley, where Allon's original plan was carried out, albeit the harsh climate limited the number of Jews who came to live there so that it fell far short of the government's expectations; and albeit that they never succeeded in building a proper economic infrastructure for themselves but remained dependent on handouts from the Zionist Federation. At one point we find Allon and Eshkol discussing whether the corridor leading to the Valley should be six miles wide or only three.[17] Since the goal was peace with Jordan, one can only call the debate surrealistic; it is as if Israel had never heard of the U.N. Charter (which, however, it had signed) which prohibits the use of force for annexing territory. As countless overt and covert meetings with local notables as well as King Hussein made clear, there was never the slightest chance of the settlements being recognized by the Palestinians, or by the neighboring Arab states, or by anybody else. In this sense the political logic behind them was always questionable. All too often their real rationale was to build a constituency that would make it harder for Israel's own leaders to surrender the Territories. Those leaders acted like the man who cut off his penis to ensure his wife did not enjoy sex; and, like that man, they have succeeded in achieving their purpose.

Do the settlements make any real contribution to Israel's defense and, if so, just what does that contribution consist of? Far from starting in 1967, this question has a long history, going back to the early days of Zionism when the first Jewish settlements had been designed with an eye to defending against what, at that time, was known as "the tent-dwelling sons of Yishmael."[18] During the 1948 War of Independence, many of the then-existing collective settlements were fortified and played a role in holding up the Arab invaders.[19] This was particularly true of six kibbutzim, to wit: Mishmar Haemek (on the southern edge of the Plain of Esraelon), where the "Arab Salvation Army" had been beaten; Dgania (on the shores of Lake Galilee), where the Syrians had been repulsed; Gesher and Tirat Zvi (on the Jordan River not far south of Dgania), where the Iraqi Army had been halted before taking another route further to the south; Negba (south of Tel Aviv), where the last Egyptian offensive was stopped; and Ramat Rachel (on the outskirts of Jerusalem), where another Egyptian column spent itself. Of these, Dgania and Negba were especially important, entering the national consciousness as the places whose inhabitants had "saved" Israel. What made the issue even more interesting was that most kibbutzim belonged to the left wing of the political spectrum and, in particular, MAPAI. In this way it was linked to the ideology that justified that Party's rule; the kibbutzim and other collective settlements had saved Israel in the past and would do so again if the need arose.

Some of the stories of heroism were not unfounded. Thus, at Dgania, the Syrian tank that spearheaded the attack penetrated to the very heart of the kibbutz before being stopped by a Molotov cocktail. Fifty-five years later its remains are still on display; the other five kibbutzim also set up museums, or, at the very least, war memorials. Still, in the end all five settlements held out not just because of their inhabitants' determination to resist at all cost but because they had been heavily reinforced by such other forces as were available at the time. To single out Dgania again, it was primarily a PALMACH battalion plus some field artillery (two antiquated mountain guns brought up at the last moment) and not the inhabitants who, after half a day's fighting, forced the Syrians to beat a retreat. A fortiori in the years after 1967, to expect the settlements to withstand an attack by a regular Arab army with its artillery and tanks was simply preposterous. Nor were the authorities in any doubt about the matter. The very first thing Dayan, learning of the coming Syrian offensive early on the morning of 6 October 1973, did was to order the civilian population of the Golan Heights evacuated;[20] to the extent that doing so took effort and organization, the settlements actually hindered the IDF's operations. The lesson was learnt and, after the War was ended, the few settlements that existed in the Sinai were simply dismantled. So much for using them as a defensive "asset" and resisting an invasion, a point, incidentally, which even the hardest of hard-liners came to concede.[21]

Contrary to the expectations of some, moreover, the settlements did little to combat terrorists. Not only did their presence act as a provocation to the other side, but the more of them that were built the more they and their inhabitants were turned into targets. Instead of guarding, they had to be put under guard, in which respect they were little different from any other Jewish towns and villages from 1948 on. Some of the guards were provided by the settlers themselves, in the form of hired personnel and vigilantes, but the great majority consisted of regular troops detailed for the purpose. This compelled the IDF to divide into penny packets, dissipated its strength, and cost it a bundle. Many settlements are so small, so isolated, and so awkwardly located on remote mountaintops, that almost as many men are needed to protect them as there are people living in them; two-fifths of them were built on sites not covered by any security map submitted by any Israeli leader. Instead of being located in the Jordan Valley, as Allon wanted, or on the watershed, as Dayan (and, many years later, Ariel Sharon) did, about two-thirds are scattered either along the western mountain slopes or, which is stranger still, along the eastern ones. Seen from a security point of view, indeed, the entire map of settlement hardly makes sense at all.[22]

While these questions were being debated and, in a manner of speaking, settled, the IDF itself was also moving into the Territories to garrison them and prepare for another war. In time, "closed" military areas and settlements together took up 60 percent of all the land; even the 40 percent that remained was so badly fragmented into penny packets as to make their inhabitants resemble "drugged bugs in a bottle" (General Rafael Eytan, IDF Chief of Staff, 1978–1982). Both settlements and bases implied access roads—their total length is now over 600 miles, dirt roads and goat tracks not included—water pipes, electricity lines, telephone links, supply dumps, fences, and so on. All these elements fed and reinforced each other; like Topsy, the Israeli presence grew and grew. Take the road going down from Jerusalem to Jericho. Until the late 1970s the country through which it runs was still almost entirely deserted and inhabited, to the extent that it was inhabited at all, only by a few Bedouin who left the Negev on a seasonal basis, lived in tents, and raised a few miserable goats. By now it bristles with the signs of human (Jewish) settlement; including electricity poles, billboards, gas stations, army bases, villages, and one entire town—Ma'ale Edumim—linked to Jerusalem both by a large interchange and by a tunnel under Mount Scopus. Whereas, before 1967, the Golan Heights were shrouded in darkness as night fell, now each evening they come alive with blazing lights along their entire length. To justify its policy, or lack of it, the Government could claim, with some reason, that any public attempt to separate what was essential from what was not would only weaken Israel's position by serving as a starting point in eventual negotiations. Hence it deliberately avoided making a decision; and the longer it procrastinated, the more difficult developments on the ground made it to find a solution.

After the 1973 War had come and gone, it could be interpreted in one of two ways. To some it proved that not even "defensible" borders made Israel safe against surprise attack. After all, the War in question had been the first one Israel did not win hands down; hence the idea of relying on such borders for security was fundamentally false or, at best, incomplete. The more land Israel conquered, the more it would have to conquer in order to render its conquests defensible, particularly if it went ahead and settled them as well. The outcome was a vicious cycle that could end, if at all, when Israel had conquered Mars to defend its settlements on the moon. Clearly this was absurd, and clearly a way out had to be found. In the words of then former foreign minister Abba Eban,[23] the concept of secure borders should be extended to include such nonmilitary elements as buffer zones, bilateral security arrangements, and so on; the more such elements were included, the less the need for territory.

Another reason why defensible borders had not come up to expectations was because the IDF had fought the 1973 War in the wrong way, militarily speaking. At the heart of the problem was Israel's fear, which was certainly well founded, that the Security Council would order a cease-fire "in place" as soon as the Arabs had registered some initial military success. Hence, beginning during the term of office of Chief of Staff Haim Bar Lev (1968–1972) it was decided not to use the strategic depth the IDF now possessed to engage in maneuver warfare. Instead of enticing the enemy forward with a view to surrounding and destroying him later, on both fronts Israel tried to hold on to every inch of land it had conquered. By so doing it made a mockery of the strategic depth it possessed—all that depth did was to make the supply lines longer than they needed to be—and turned the Territories from an asset into a self-made trap. One where, during the early days of the war, fortifications were surrounded or overrun, hundreds of troops either killed or forced to surrender, and entire armored brigades frittered away in attempts to rescue them that were as futile as they were brave.

However, the idea that "defensible borders" had failed was only taken up by a small minority. The majority took council of their fears, and understandably so; nobody who lived in Israel on that fateful day, 6 October, when, coming out of a blue sky on the holiest of all holy days, the sirens started howling, will ever forget the shock. From a future minister of defense, Professor Moshe Arens, down, they saw the War as a vindication of "defensible" borders, which, they claimed, were the one thing that had stood between Israel and destruction.[24] This interpretation made them even more determined to hold on, if not to everything then certainly to much of the Occupied Territories. Certainly as long as peace was not achieved; and, many would say, even at the expense of not doing whatever possible to achieve it. During the years before 1967 the army's doctrine had centered on the impracticality of mounting a military defense and the consequent need for launching a preemptive strike into enemy territory. Now, by contrast, it called for using the air force and standing army to "absorb" an enemy offensive while simultaneously mobilizing the reserves in preparation for a large-scale counterattack. In the mid-1970s this approach led to fortifications being built even where they had never previously existed, as along the Jordan Valley.

Since strategy was very much in dispute, the one thing everybody could agree on was the need for a tremendous military buildup; never again was a situation to recur when just three divisions, two of them badly attrited by futile counterattacks, had stood between the Egyptians and Tel Aviv. Most of the money came from the U.S., which increased its aid ninefold from the pre-War figure of $250 million to over $2 billion a year. Israel itself also girded its economic loins until one quarter of the entire industrial workforce found itself engaged in the manufacture of arms, causing the IDF's order of battle to more than double and its arsenal to grow in proportion. As Weizman wrote in his memoirs, when he took over as minister of defense in 1977—he had doffed his uniform eight years previously—he could scarcely believe his eyes at the awesome array that greeted him.[25] Never in history did such a small country grow such sharp teeth;[26] as used to be said at the time, had China wanted to deploy as many tanks per capita as Israel did, it would have had to acquire at least a million of them.

Side by side with the quantitative buildup there was a massive influx of modern weapon systems never previously seen in the Middle East. The most important ones were an entirely new generation of attack aircraft as superior to their predecessors as motor cars were to horse-drawn carts. Next came attack helicopters, tanks, very large numbers of armored personnel carriers and self-propelled artillery tubes, antitank and antiaircraft, missiles, missile boats that kept growing larger and larger until they developed into small frigates, and short-range, tactical, Lance surface-to-surface missiles. As significant, new transport aircraft and an air-to-air refueling capability for the first time gave the Air Force more than a purely regional capability; until it could reach as far as the Straits of Bab El Mandeb in the south and Tunisia in the west.

To top it all, foreign sources began speaking of three different kinds of strategic surface-to-surface missiles (Jericho I, II, and III). The last-named was an ICBM capable of lifting a satellite into orbit, a feat first achieved in 1987; the second was easily capable of delivering a warhead to every capital within a thousand miles. A few highly successful IDF operations, particularly the brilliant 1976 rescue of the hostages at Entebbe Airport, Uganda, helped. By the late 1970s the existential fears that had been roused by the 1973 War were largely gone, so much so that youngsters born after that date find it very hard to understand what living in Israel before their time was like. Their place was taken by a feeling of self-confidence, even arrogance; shortly after taking over as minister of defense in 1981, Ariel Sharon went so far as to claim that, from Morocco to the Persian Gulf, there was not a single force capable of stopping the IDF.[27] That confidence, in turn, was one of the factors that helped nudge the Government, as well as the public on which it rested, towards the possibility of peace.

In May 1977, the defeat of Labor and the rise to power of Menahem Begin's right wing Likud Government marked another stage in the process. Whatever the popular feeling, until then Israel had been governed by Labor politicians such as Ben Gurion, Eshkol, Meir, and Meir's successor, Rabin. Though claiming to be socialist, on the whole they had the backing of Israel's more prosperous, better-educated classes. Their worldview was secular and their approach to the problem of the Occupied Territories, including the West Bank, essentially pragmatic. Certainly they did not see the 1949 armistice lines as sacrosanct; on the other hand, though much more flexible in principle than in practice, they honestly looked for some "balanced compromise" (Allon again) which, they fondly hoped, would be acceptable to both sides.

The country's new rulers were a different kettle of fish. A rabid nationalist who tended to be carried away by his own oratory, Begin had opposed every "concession" Israel ever made. In 1970 he even resigned from a National Unity Government simply because Ms. Meir had uttered the word "withdrawal" in a speech she made in Parliament; later, too, he gave Meir and Rabin hell. As he himself put it, he and his party had been elected "by those who are poor and those who believe." Sectarian politics apart, almost the only thing they had going for them was the fact that many of those who voted for them were afraid of Arabs and hated them; that was true then and remains true today. Before long he launched a massive effort at populating the Territories with Jews, causing the latter's number to increase from 9,000 to 100,000 in only five years. More to emphasize his determination than for any practical reason, he also passed a law that formally annexed the Golan Heights. Notwithstanding that he must have realized that the move stood no chance of being recognized by anybody, Israel's closest allies included; and notwithstanding that it would only serve to alienate world opinion. Yet much as he was given to grand gestures, Begin was enough of a realist to see that Israel could not retain all its gains forever, and that compromises would have to be made. It was in order to keep the Golan Heights and the West Bank, not as a first step towards an agreement with all of Israel's neighbors, that he finally prepared to sign the 1979 Camp David Peace Accords. Three years later the IDF withdrew, and the whole of the Sinai went back to Egypt.

As the invasion of Lebanon was to show, Begin's understanding of defense affairs had been formed during his kindergarten days and had not developed since. Like his mentor, Zeev Jabotinsky, all he really cared about was parades, if possible ones at which he himself could take the salute. Nineteen hundred eighty-two years into the Christian calendar, he still wondered whether guerrillas might have machine guns. Apparently the model he had in mind was the Poland of his youth; a place where such weapons had been few and far between. The same could not be said of his most important collaborators, i.e. Moshe Dayan, who was serving as foreign minister, and former Air Force Commander and Deputy Chief of Staff Ezer Weizman, who was appointed minister of defense. Both men were world-renowned experts in the field, fully capable of forming views and articulating them. More remarkable still, both had long been known for their hawkish views. Specifically it was Dayan who insisted that Israel should settle the northeastern Sinai, a district over which he had quarreled with Meir's powerful minister of the treasury, Pinhas Sapir, and which he thought was needed in order to permanently separate the Gaza Strip from Egypt. Weizman, though he was Dayan's brother-in-law, probably owed his failure to reach the post of chief of staff to the fact that he was regarded as a fire-eater. In 1970, by which time he was no longer in uniform but serving as minister of transportation, he had been one of the very few Israelis who proclaimed the "War of Attrition" a defeat for Israel; he even demanded that hostilities be resumed. Briefly, for more than ten years after 1967, both men had often insisted on the need for a "secure" border, and neither would have risked returning to the old one if they had considered it "indefensible." The more so because, at the time the Agreements were made, there was no knowing whether Egypt would stick to them or not.[28]

In the event, what took place was just the opposite. As peace took hold, the share of defense out of Israel's total resources—both domestic and foreign—declined from 31 percent in 1974–1976 to 22 percent in 1977–1981.[29] Not only did the IDF demolish the military infrastructure, but the Peninsula was demilitarized. The cities along the Canal were rebuilt and repopulated, itself a powerful argument to deter Egypt from launching another war in which hundreds of thousands of its citizens might once again be made homeless and an investment of billions go to waste. The Agreements only permitted a token Egyptian force to cross the Canal; and even that force could do no more than police an area twenty miles to the east of it. Though the "warm" peace many Israelis hoped for has not materialized—some would say it was destroyed by Israeli military actions in Lebanon, the Territories, and elsewhere—the Egyptians, according to a former Israeli ambassador in Cairo, have observed the military Agreement "to the last grain of sand." If anything it was Israeli pilots who sometimes violated it. First they "accidentally" penetrated into Egyptian air space, and then they offered lame explanations for their actions;[30] whether this was done in quest of intelligence, or to test the other side's reactions, or for some other purpose, only those who gave the orders know. In any case, about a hundred miles of open desert now separated Israel's border from the nearest Egyptian forces, their air force included. Any possibility of a surprise attack was ruled out both by American early warning stations and by the IDF's own. While individual vehicles could cross the Peninsula in a few hours, it was estimated that building up a strong force on Israel's border would take from six to eight days; more than enough time for Israel to mobilize its forces and put them where they had to be. Israel became easier to defend then it had been when the two sides had stood eyeball to eyeball with only the "best antitank trench in the world" to keep them apart.

Twenty years later, few people can remember when, to quote Allon, "unquestionable control" over the northeastern Sinai, the Straits, the Corridor leading to them, and other parts of the Sinai were considered so "critical" to Israel's defense that keeping them was preferable to peace. Yet, at the time he published his plan in the world's most prestigious foreign-affairs magazine, Allon was serving as foreign minister under that great peacemaker, Rabin; compared to some others, both in his own party and in the opposition, he was considered a dove! On the other hand, Ezer Weizman in his memoirs calls the ensuing situation "ideal" both for the Egyptians and for Israel.[31] Since his own career included two major wars in which the Israeli Air Force had chopped up the Egyptian forces in the Sinai, he ought to know. Dayan, too, considered peace with Egypt a cornerstone of Israeli security; during his last days he was much concerned with the need to prevent it from falling apart. None of these developments had any effect on Israel's northern and eastern frontiers which, in spite of countless more or less serious attempts at negotiation, have remained as they were. Almost all Israelis would like to see the conflict with Syria terminated, and repeated polls have shown that many of them are prepared to pay a high price for reaching that goal.[32] Nevertheless, to this day scarcely any public debate has taken place as to just how important the Golan Heights are for the country's defense, let alone as to whether it might be defended without them, and, if so, how. The same is even more true of the Gaza Strip and, above all, the West Bank. Looking back on the controversy between Dayan and Allon as to what parts of the Occupied Territories were the most important, and taking into account military-technological developments since then, one can only wonder which of them had right on his side. Perhaps both did; perhaps, neither.

As is well known, in the aftermath of the 1870–1871 Franco-Prussian War the Prussian Chief of Staff, Helmut von Moltke, demanded the annexation of Alsace-Lorraine so as to prevent any future French invasion of Germany and, in the end, succeeded in getting his way against Bismarck's opposition. As is less well known Karl Marx, who was no military expert, jokingly asked his friend Friedrich Engels, who was, whether the war had not proved how easy it was for Germany to invade France.[33] Born out of terrible fear, and later reinforced by the messianic feelings that the War itself generated, the mental processes which, starting soon after the smashing victory of 1967, led to the belief that Israel was "indefensible" from within its old borders were no doubt human, all too human. The more so because it was adopted and supported by most of the leading military experts of the time; and the more so because of the even greater fear generated by the surprise attack of 6 October 1973. This, however, does not mean that the conclusions to which they led are necessarily right. The more so because, at least as far as the public domain is concerned, those conclusions have never been thoroughly examined or an alternative to them proposed.

Supposing Israel withdraws to the pre-1967 borders or to something so close to them as to make little difference, strategically—how will its defense be affected? To answer this question, let us start by focusing on the grand strategic level where political and military considerations meet. As we saw, before 1967 Israel's geographic and demographic resources were dwarfed by those of its neighbors. After 1967, though the territory under its control quadrupled, that territory was still dwarfed by that of its neighbors. Including all the Occupied Territories, Israel now controlled about 31,000 square miles of land. By contrast Egypt alone, even without the Sinai Peninsula, still measured 360,000 square miles. Taking the other Arab countries into consideration, so great was the disparity that it could hardly even be expressed in percentage points; to find Israel on a small-scale map of the Middle East one must use a magnifying glass.

The same applies to the demographic balance which, in spite of considerable Jewish immigration, has remained very much as it had been. At the time of writing some 5.4 million Jews—6.7 million Israelis, if one counts over a million Arab Israelis—are facing almost 90 million Arabs in Egypt, Jordan, Lebanon, and Syria. These figures do not include other Arab—let alone Moslem—countries from Iraq to Morocco. Almost all of them are hostile to Israel, and only three—Egypt, Jordan, and Mauritania—so much as have diplomatic relations with it. Most have a decades-long history of boycotting Israeli trade, if not always de facto then certainly de jure; several have also sent expeditionary forces to wage war against it and/or contributed money to the noble cause of combating Zionism. Far from alleviating these problems, the 1967 War aggravated them. First, psychologically speaking, it was as hard for the Egyptians to watch their enemies washing their feet in the Suez Canal as it was for the Syrians to see the IDF's antennae on the Golan Heights. Second, the situation was complicated still further by the fact that Mount Temple with its mosques, the second most holy Moslem site, was now in Jewish hands. Third, and perhaps even more important, the War saddled Israel with a large, and increasingly hostile, Arab population within its borders. In that sense, too, all it did was to make a bad situation worse. As Eshkol is supposed to have said: With such a homely bride, who wants the dowry?

True, Israeli forces were now positioned much closer to three Arab capitals—to wit, Cairo, Amman, and Damascus. Of these, the second and especially the third were within fairly easy striking range of the IDF's ground forces. Still, geography is not the only factor. The extent of the change should not be exaggerated; as the invasion of Lebanon was to prove, for the Israeli canary to capture an Arab cat, in the form of a capital, is not a good idea. In part, this was because cities have a habit of swallowing up vast numbers of troops which Israel, depending on re-servists to fill its army and extremely sensitive to casualties, could not afford. In part, it was because such an occupation would not necessar-ily enable Israel to dictate the peace any more than the U.S. having oc-cupied Baghdad in 2003, was able to put an end to terrorism in Iraq.

The proof of this particular pudding was in the eating. In 1983 Lebanon was governed, to the extent it was governed at all, by President Amin Jumayel. On 17 May, hard-pressed by Israel's Minister of Defense Ariel Sharon, Jumayel *did* sign something like a formal peace treaty. At the time Sharon hailed it as "a huge achievement"; soon enough, how-ever, it proved not to be worth the paper on which it had been written, and today few people even remember it ever existed. Besides, occupy-ing an Arab capital was very likely to bring on diplomatic complica-tions, as also happened in 1983 when an international force was sent to protect Beirut—against whom was not clear—and came within a hair of trading shots with the Israeli Army there. In these and other ways, Israel's occupation of the Territories has done little to ease the grand strategic handicap under which its defense has labored and will labor as long as there is such a thing as an Arab World.[1] The opposite is also true. Getting rid of the Territories will make it necessary to modify Israel's grand strategy in detail. However, it will not aggravate the handicap to any great extent; the more so because the very size of the World in question means that important parts of it are far, far away.

In fact, it was precisely the grand-strategic handicap—in plain words, the disparity in resources—which, in the years before 1967, caused Israel to base its defense on a preemptive strike against any Arab country that might threaten it. During the decades since then, its ability to launch such a strike has been affected in several ways.[2] On the one hand there are developments in international law, as well as the growing inclination of the Security Council to rule over war and peace. As a result, a strike is now likely to be regarded with even less favor by the international community than before. Note America's failure to gain permission to attack Iraq in 2003; to invert the Latin saying, what Jupiter is not allowed to do is even less permissible for the bull. On the other, Israel now enjoys tolerable relations with some of the world's more important powers, such as China and India, which until the 1990s did not even recognize its existence and did what they could to obstruct it—although, if truth be said, that did not amount to much. For what it is worth, should Israel once again find itself in a tight spot there is no reason to worry that those two countries will automatically align themselves with its enemies. In the case of India the opposite may well be the case. Tel Aviv now has an ongoing strategic relationship with New Delhi, one that includes arms sales, an exchange of intelligence, counterterrorism, and much else.[3]

Much more important, the Soviet Union no longer exists. From 1943 on the U.S.S.R., looking to the end of the war and hoping to weaken the Anglo-American position in the Middle East, started voicing its support for Jewish immigration to the Land of Israel. In November 1947 it used its United Nations seat to vote in favor of the establishment of Israel and put pressure on other nations to do the same; six months later it granted de jure recognition even before the U.S. did. Soon afterwards it permitted its Czech client to sell weapons, such as machine guns, artillery, and fighter aircraft. But for those weapons the Jewish State might not have survived its first months; for many years thereafter, the IDF's standard-issue, German-made rifles were known as "Czech." Good relations between the two sides lasted until 1950. The outbreak of the Korean War caused Ben Gurion to cast his country's lot with the West;[4] the way he saw it, should World War III break out the West would gain command of the Mediterranean and be in a position to resupply Israel, whereas the East would not. Stalin's response was the so-called "Doctors Plot," as well as severing diplomatic ties. Though diplomatic ties were resumed after the dictator's death, the original good relationship between the two countries was never restored and, from then on, Soviet propaganda increasingly turned "Zionism" into a synonym for anything evil.

Still, the great turning point in Soviet-Arab relations had to wait until the summer of 1955, when the Kremlin undertook to provide Egypt with weapons under the so-called "Czech arms deal."[5] Originally the Soviet motive in entering the deal was not so much to help Egypt's ruler, Gamal Abdul Nasser, confront Israel as to keep him from joining the pro-Western Baghdad Pact which was then being formed. Things acquired their own momentum, though, and from then until 1973 inclusive the U.S.S.R. found itself closely allied with the "radical" Arab States: including, besides Egypt, Israel's sworn enemies Syria, and, from 1958 on, Iraq. After the 1967 War the Kremlin again severed its diplomatic ties with Israel and made its East European satellites (with the exception of Romania) do the same. This situation was to last for over twenty years.

Though Egypt, then under Anwar Sadat, became an American ally after 1973, Soviet support for Syria, Iraq and, from 1969 on, Libya continued until the end of the Cold War. For many years Moscow sold— one is tempted to say, gave—its clients so many weapons as to make them bristle; some proved beyond the Arabs' capacity to absorb, and they ended up rusting in the desert. For example, after its defeat in June 1967 it took the Egyptian Army only a year and a half to reequip its forces, though restoring their fighting spirit and self-confidence was more difficult. The Syrian Army was not far behind; with the weapons came on-the-spot training as well as countless visits by Arab officers to Soviet military colleges. Looking back, had it not been for this assistance then probably most Arab armed forces would never have been in a position to fight anyone except their own people; let alone do so effectively and on any scale.

Nor was Soviet assistance to the Arabs limited exclusively to training and arms. Both in November 1956 and in October 1973 the Kremlin threatened, or seemed to threaten, Israel, with military intervention as first Mr. Khruschev and then Mr. Brezhnev rattled their nuclear missiles. In the winter and spring of 1970 it actually did intervene in the so-called War of Attrition. First, 20,000 Soviet "advisers" arrived in Egypt. They were integrated into every unit down to battalion level and, which was more important, manned the antiaircraft defenses along the Suez Canal; until, along with those deployed against the U.S.A. in Vietnam, those defenses became the most powerful on earth. When that still did not prove enough to halt the rain of bombs coming down on Egypt, Moscow sent its own pilots to fly missions against the Israelis over the Suez Canal. They turned out to be second-rate, and four of them were shot down. However, that was scant consolation to Israel, which feared that full-scale military action was in the making and worried lest Washington would not come to its aid.[6]

By 1982, when Israel was preparing to launch its Lebanese adventure, the Soviet Union had run into serious difficulties in Afghanistan and the prospect of military intervention on its part had grown quite remote. Still it could not be altogether ignored; indeed, the Kremlin published a statement that was clearly meant as a warning to Israel.[7] This may explain why Sharon, who was in charge, ordered his commanders to stay away from the border with Syria and refrain from crossing it under any circumstances. They were to limit themselves to defeating the Syrian forces in Lebanon;[8] there was to be no repetition of the events of 1967 when Israel's push towards Damascus has caused the Soviets to threaten it in no uncertain terms.[9] Fear of Soviet intervention may also have been one reason why such huge forces were used against such a weak opponent in such a small, overcrowded country. The total was six and a half divisions, equal to the IDF's entire order of battle in 1973; two more divisions were stationed on the Golan Heights, ready to repel a Syrian attack. Had the Soviets wanted to interfere, then doing so would have required more than a token force.

Just nine years later, the situation changed fundamentally as the Soviet Union imploded. Politically and militarily, its Russian successor is much weaker. The Ukraine and other southern republics having regained their independence, Russia is also much further away from the Middle East. Nor is it nearly as involved in what goes on in that part of the world.[10] Having lost the Crimea and its naval bases on the Black Sea coast, geo-politically speaking Russia has been rolled back approximately to where it was before Katherine the Great came to power in 1762; Arab leaders are as capable of appreciating these facts as is anyone else. The mighty Soviet battle fleets—at peak they numbered as many as sixty to seventy ships, including both a Marine landing force and a naval air component—that used to cruise the Mediterranean during most of the 1970s and 1980s are gone. So are the bases in Egypt and Syria that provided them with logistic support, repair facilities, and so on; they are probably gone for good, and certainly for as long as anyone can foresee. Having freed themselves from their desire to serve as a beacon for the toiling masses everywhere, the new rulers in the Kremlin do not feel duty-bound to rescue the Arabs each time the latter ask them to; the more so because some Arab states support the rebels in Chechnya. It is true that, as the running dispute over alleged Russian nuclear assistance to Iran shows, Moscow may not always see eye to eye with Jerusalem. Still, on the whole relations between the two sides have been fair. In December 1995 they even signed an agreement to cooperate in military-industrial matters; the change from the Cold War could not have been greater.

While all this was going on, Israel's own armed forces have grown to the point where, in purely operational terms if not in point of staying power, they are now probably the third or fourth most powerful on earth. For years after Israel feared that Britain would once again confront it with an ultimatum as it had done in 1949. After 1956, at the latest, all of this went by the board; nowadays only one country, i.e. the United States, still has what it takes.[11] In the past America, confronted by large-scale Israeli offensive operations, has reacted now in one way, now in another. In November 1956 it was President Eisenhower's retroactive veto, along with Soviet threats, that forced the Israelis and their British and French allies to relinquish the gains they had made in the Suez Campaign. During the crisis of May–June 1967 the U.S. then under President Johnson, hesitated for weeks before it made up its mind, but ended by permitting Israel to launch a preventive war against its neighbors and, especially, Egypt.[12] In January 1970 Rabin, who was then Israel's ambassador in Washington, D.C., claimed that the Nixon Administration welcomed the start of Israel's "deep bombing" campaign against Egypt.[13] The claim may not have been entirely true; in any case the U.S. did provide its protégé with the Phantom aircraft without which the campaign would have been impossible. In September of the same year the two countries engaged in what was perhaps their closest cooperation ever. Standing shoulder to shoulder they threatened to attack Syria should the latter not halt its drive into Jordan; as Israel put its own forces on alert, the U.S. deployed the Sixth Fleet.[14]

In October 1973 it was primarily the need to placate the Americans that prevented Israel, then ruled by Ms. Meir, from launching a pre-emptive strike against Egypt and Syria. Within two days, it was rewarded for its restraint. First Washington, confronting Moscow, prevented the Security Council from passing a cease-fire resolution that Assad demanded[15] and which would have left much of the Golan Heights in Syrian hands. Next, President Nixon ordered the airlift to start, encouraging Israel, providing it with some badly needed items, and above all, signaling to all the world that he would not permit America's ally to fall. Third, he put his own armed forces on nuclear alert, thus countering what, at the time, looked like a serious Soviet threat against Israel.[16] In June 1981 the Reagan Administration publicly condemned the destruction of the Iraqi nuclear reactor by Israel while praising it in private. Scarcely had another year passed, and the same administration permitted the invasion of Lebanon to go ahead.[17] Finally, in January-February 1991, Washington did demand that Jerusalem refrain from retaliating against Saddam Hussein's missiles. But only because its own armed forces were already doing what they could to find and destroy those very missiles; and only because it believed, with very good reason, that an Israeli strike might hamper their efforts by creating difficulties with the Arab members of the Coalition. In the event Israel did hold its fire but, as it had often done in the past, hastened to extract a quid pro quo. This time it consisted of Patriot Missiles sent to protect the country and left there after the war was over; in 2003, too, Jerusalem used the Iraqi crisis to extract military and economic aid.

The conclusion from all this might well be that, taking 1967 as our starting point, policy makers in Washington have urged their client to exercise restraint on some occasions but not on others. Very often the precise line they would take could not be predicted but depended on the circumstances of the moment. At times Israel was simply waging America's wars by proxy, teaching some of the Arabs—and, through them, their patrons in the Kremlin—a lesson that the White House wanted them to learn. At others, America's refusal to rein in Israel was designed to leverage the Arab world by showing that it, and it alone, was able to pull that rein should it want to. Sometimes the Americans held the Israelis back, as happened in 1967 when a small IDF unit crossed the Jordan River into the East Bank—without orders, it was later claimed—and also in 1973 when they refused permission to starve out the surrounded Egyptian Third Army. On other occasions too the U.S. has been paying the Arabs in Israeli coin. Though doing so has never been a consistent policy, it is almost certain to happen again.

Whatever their differences, at a more fundamental level the two countries have been marching side by side at least since President Kennedy, having given up hope of drawing the "radical" Arabs back into the fold, began building the foundations for an alliance between them. He ended the unofficial arms embargo his predecessor had imposed, agreed to sell Israel weapons or permit other countries to do so, and promised to maintain the military balance between it and the Arabs.[18] During the forty years since then their relationship has been consolidated. The Reagan Administration in particular tended to see Israel as a strategic asset, and was the first to sign Memoranda of Understanding with Jerusalem.[19] Since then the number and significance of the agreements has increased as the two countries cooperated in many fields and as American military equipment was pre-positioned on Israeli territory. Each time a crisis breaks out, high-level consultations take place; the more serious it is, the more likely it is to result in more American aid in the form of weapons, money, or both.

The process is facilitated by the fact that Israel is, after all, a democracy, and, to that extent, has more in common with the U.S. than do some other Middle Eastern countries with their thuggish leaders and closed, totalitarian regimes. Another factor that emerged during the 1980s and 1990s was a growing community of interests in controlling or confronting some of the more radical elements in the Arab world.

Generally speaking, the more extreme any Arab regime and the more it tends to support terrorism, the more likely Washington and Jerusalem are to team up against it and cooperate to clip its wings. The latest to experience this was Syria's Bashir Assad. In the summer of 2003 he found himself caught between the American hammer and the Israeli anvil; forcing him to redeploy some of his forces in Lebanon or, at least, pretend he did.

Conversely, America's internal politics constrain its ability to take on Israel head-on. The first time this became clear was during the early 1960s when Kennedy tried, but failed, to make Ben Gurion give up his country's fledgling weapons program by putting it under the control of the International Nuclear Energy Commission. Partly because he was less interested in nonproliferation, partly because he had other matters to preoccupy him, his successor Lyndon Johnson did not even try. Determined not to let this problem come between them, he and Levy Eshkol ended up by working out a modus vivendi instead. Under its terms, the Israelis promised not to tell and the Americans not to see what was going on, even during the visits that their scientists paid to the Dimona reactor.[20] From then to the present both sides have stuck to the bargain. Even if, as may have been the case, keeping silent has cost Israel some of its deterrent power; and even if the Americans had to deny the evidence of their own satellites when Israel allegedly conducted a test in 1979.[21]

To some extent, the close relations between the two countries reflect the influence of the Jewish lobby and, in particular AIPAC (American-Israeli Public Affairs Committee). However, the lobby's power is liable to be exaggerated by Israel's enemies, both in the U.S. itself and abroad. During the first decades of its existence AIPAC had little influence, and it was only in the 1980s that it became a powerhouse. Even now it is but one lobby among many others; some of those others, notably the one that represents the oil companies, are both anti-Israeli and at least as well organized and financed as the Jews are. Jewish

Americans only number about 2 percent of America's population—6 out of almost 300 million. Of those, probably fewer than half are committed Zionists in the sense that they support Israel in any way.

Some Jews, particularly on the intellectual left, want nothing to do with Israel, which they see as a colonialist and even criminal state. Others are in no position to influence elections more than anyone else; finally, as often happens to lobbies, there have been times when AIPAC has acted more as a conduit for conveying Washington's wishes to Jerusalem than the other way around.[22] On both ends of the political spectrum, the right and the left, there are some Americans who like to fantasize about the Zionist Occupied Government, popularly known as ZOG. However, at the most senior level President Bush's foreign and defense policy advisers do not include a single Jew. Not only do many of its members have close ties with the oil industry, but two of them, Vice President Richard Cheney and Secretary of State Colin Powell used to be members of the Senior Bush's Administration back in 1988–1992 which, some people in Jerusalem believe, was the least pro-Israeli one in four decades.

More important, between about 1998 and 2002, has been the rise of the Evangelical Right on the one hand and of the Neo-Conservative Movement on the other. The former are clearly distinct from mainstream Protestants, on the one hand, and Catholics on the other. Closely associated with the Republican Party, many of them support Israel on mystic grounds. Some of them entertain the not-so-secret hope of sending the Jews there one day. Once this has happened, they are supposed to convert to Christianity and help bring along the Second Coming of Christ;[23] as so often, philo- and anti-Semitic feelings can produce strange bedfellows. The latter are mainly a group of intellectuals among whom, as it happens, there are many Jews. Some Neo-Conservatives have their origins in the extreme left, others in the radical right. Their principal concern is with America's position in the world, how to strengthen it, and how to safeguard it against what, on

the basis of historical comparisons with previous empires, they consider its inevitable decline. Most see Israel as an asset in the global
power game, and that part of it which is directed against Islamic terrorism in particular. At a less elevated, more popular level it may be fortunate for Israel that many Americans who are not intellectuals often
have an instinctive dislike for Arabs, an emotion which the events of
9-11 and their sequels have done nothing to obviate.

As the ascent and, some would say, incipient decline of the Neo-
Conservatives itself illustrates, the balance of forces in Washington,
D.C., is anything but fixed, and is likely to change further in years to
come. Surely new interest groups will rise and form new coalitions in
their bids for power; for example, not every administration will owe as
much to AIPAC and the Jews as Bill Clinton did. Nor will future presi-
dents necessarily choose to confront parts of the Arab world head-on as
George W. Bush has done. Instead, they may follow other policies that
will not be as welcome in Jerusalem, whether in regard to the Territories, or to nuclear proliferation, or anything else. Still, anyone who expects the U.S. to do to Israel what it has done to Serbia or Iraq—and
may conceivably do to Iran or North Korean—might as well be baying
at the moon. This is obvious from the fact that, over the last thirty-six
years and in spite of countless disagreements between the two countries, the U.S. has always refused to apply pressure that would have
forced Israel to relinquish land except on terms that Jerusalem felt were
acceptable. The outcome, far from weakening Israel, has been to
strengthen it. Once they had been signed, the peace agreements with
Egypt and Jordan became cornerstones of its security; American aid
has also played a decisive role in enabling Israel to become by far the
strongest military power in the Middle East.

To look at it in a different way, Israel is not simply a client of the U.S.,
always ready to obey the latter's commands. Owing to its dependence on
American financial and military aid, Jerusalem is likely to listen to its Big
Brother in most issues that are placed on the table. This is particularly

true of those that Washington indicates are critically important to it; a good recent example is the decision not to sell China the Israeli Air Force's Falcon Advanced Warning and Control System (AWACS).[24] There are, however, certain limits to this willingness. In the past, Washington has often expressed its frustration at how little influence $3 billion a year buys in Jerusalem. Think of President Carter's attempt to stop Prime Minister Begin from settling the Territories with massive numbers of Jews. In the end he failed; yet, with the exception of the October 1973 War, probably at no time was Israel more dependent on American support to confront what looked like a formidable Arab threat. Perhaps one should heed the words of Israel's one-time foreign minister, Abba Eban. "The capacity of small countries to assert their independent interest and judgement against those of powerful allies," he says, "is a feature of the modern diplomatic era, and the Israeli-American dialogue is merely the most conspicuous example of a general tendency."[25]

A president who owes something to the Jewish vote may want to get close to Israel, as Bill Clinton did, whereas one who does not may want to support it for other reasons, as Richard Nixon and Ronald Reagan did. A president who has the wind blowing in his back may not want to lean on Israel, as with Nixon and Reagan during their early years. One who does not may be unable to, as happened to G. W. Bush since he started sinking into the Iraqi swamp. Above all, experience since the late 1960s shows that, whenever America comes close to holding elections, both parties will outdo each other in promising Israel support. Out of every four years between presidential elections, one and a half are overshadowed by them. To say nothing of the biannual elections to Congress that take place in between; these, in a way, are even more important since it is in Congress that Israel has always found its most important backers. With one election campaign meshing almost seamlessly into the next, quite often all Israel has to do is play for time, carefully balancing between Democrats and Republicans, ingratiating itself with both, and avoiding too close a commitment to either.

Whatever happens, a situation whereby Jerusalem needs Washington as immediately and as desperately as it did during the October 1973 War is unlikely to recur. Therefore, should the former feel hard-pressed by the latter, then experience shows that it still has the option of saying no in the hope of mending fences later on. Think of Rabin first rejecting the Interim Agreement with Egypt that Henry Kissinger held out to him in the spring of 1975 and then, having watched Washington going through a period of "reassessment," signing it six months later.[26] A better example still was provided by the games Sharon played in respect to accepting, or not accepting, the so-called "Road Map" in the summer of 2003—agreeing to cooperate with the cease-fire even as he attached so many conditions to it as to almost nullify its intent. If worst comes to worst, then Israel's prime minister can resign and call for new elections. Doing so will ipso facto break up his Parliamentary majority, depriving him of freedom of action and causing any important move to be delayed by between three and six months. Some believe this was the real reason why Ben Gurion, pressured by the Kennedy Administration over the nuclear issue in 1963, chose to leave office at the time he did; if so, then looking back it worked as well as anybody could expect.

In the past, Washington itself has been well aware of these problems. Its ambassador in Tel Aviv has long acted as a sort of pro-consul, exercising oversight and gathering extremely detailed information on every aspect of Israeli life, military and civilian. From time to time it put Israel under pressure, and some of the pressure has been far from gentle; recall, besides Carter and Begin, Bush Sr. pressing Yitzhak Shamir to agree to participate in the Madrid Conference of 1991. Still, it never pushed Israel into a corner where, to quote Dayan in another context, the latter would behave like a rabid dog.[27] On at least one occasion, he himself told the then American Secretary of State, Cyrus Vance, that there were limits beyond which Israel would not go.[28]

Since then, given the disarray of the Arab World and Israel's own growing strength, if anything Jerusalem's ability to take liberties with

Washington has increased. A striking demonstration of this was provided during the economic conference held in Jordan in June 2003. Just twenty-four hours after Colin Powell "regretted" Israel's killing of a Hamas leader, he issued a "clarification" in which he explained that it was circumstances and not Israel that were subject to "regret";[29] just who and what stood behind the change is not clear. Overall, the upshot of these considerations is that Israel enjoys at least as much room for maneuver as it did during the Cold War. Should it once again go to war against one or more of its neighbors, then the risk of a Superpower confrontation and consequently of the Security Council mandating a cease-fire to avoid such a confrontation will be much smaller than it was before 1991. Jerusalem could have much greater freedom to bring its strike to fruition. If not by occupying an enemy capital and dictating peace, something that has always been beyond its reach, then at any rate by smashing the enemy's forces and occupying territory that may later be used for bargaining purposes.

Whether or not American support will continue indefinitely cannot be foreseen. At the time the Cold War waned away there was some speculation about the relationship's future; since then, owing primarily to the rise of Islamic Fundamentalism in many Arab countries, a situation whereby Washington performs a complete volte-face has become less likely rather than more. With Syria and Iran hostile and the partnership with Saudi Arabia becoming less reliable than before, the U.S. needs all the support in the Middle East it can get; nor, presumably, will internal politics permit it to radically change its policy even if it wanted to. More ominous is the possibility that the U.S. perhaps after getting bogged down in a costly guerrilla war in Iraq and failing to establish an acceptable government there, will lose its position not only in that country but in much of the rest of the Middle East as well. Such a development might also be part of a wider move towards isolationism such as some conservatives, who are the Neo-Conservatives' most vociferous critics, demand. Even if such a move proves temporary, as it always has in the past, it would deprive Israel of some, perhaps much, of the political, economic, and military support it now enjoys; leaving it adrift in a hostile Arab sea. At present such a scenario appears, if not imposible, at any rate some years away. Should it materialize, then it would provide all the more reason for Israel to rely on itself and do whatever is necessary to increase its power to the maximum possible extent. Which, of course, is just what the present study is all about.

To sum up, compared with the situation as it existed before 1967, Israel's grand strategic predicament remains the same in some ways but has undergone considerable changes in others. Some of the changes pull in one direction, others in the opposite. Depending on which is which, either they provide Jerusalem with more elbow room or decrease it. Precisely because they do pull in opposite directions, though, on the whole the least one can say is that things are no worse than they were before; in some important ways, they have become much better. Given that the disparity in size between Israel and its neighbors is as large as it is, an Israeli withdrawal from the Territories will only affect that balance to a limited extent, if at all. What it *may* do is force Israel to return to a political-strategic doctrine centering on a preemptive strike.[30] However, given developments in military technology, on which more is written below, even such a strike is likely to take a different form and give rise to less trouble.

Without a doubt, such a strike will be hard to justify in the eyes of the international community, meaning that it will carry some kind of political price, as also happened after the 1967 War, when many countries severed relations with Israel. Fortunately this is much less true in respect to the one country that matters, i.e. the United States. Should the strike be launched, then owing to the demise of the Cold War and Israel's own growing strength, there will be no outside power left to threaten Israel with military action. To that extent there is a much better chance that Israel will be permitted to go through with it instead of being forced to stop in mid-stride, as often happened in the past, something of which the Arab leaders ought to be aware. Whichever way one looks at it, the joker in the pack is the U.S.A. Though the alliance between the two countries is now several decades old, whether or not it will continue indefinitely is not clear; certainly the answer is by no means solely a function of whether the latter does or does not retain the Territories. Needless to say it is impossible to foresee the future with certainty, let alone guarantee the outcome of any situation that may arise. Much will depend on the circumstances of the moment, the personalities in power, and the way each of the parties decides to play its cards. Still, the least one can say is that there is no reason to despair.

Discussing grand strategy is one thing, preparing for war, another. Like any other state, Israel would dearly like to have allies that would come to its assistance in case of need. More than most states, it spent much of its history as an international pariah—to the point that, in all the years since it was founded, it has been perhaps the only state that has never been able to win a seat on the Security Council. Thanks partly to the collapse of the Soviet Union, partly to American support, the worst days of ostracism appear to be over and there are now many more embassies in Tel Aviv than there used to be twenty-five years ago. Still the country must prepare for war as if it were alone in the world, and indeed one declared pillar of Israeli strategy has long been that it would "never" ask others to fight for it. The question is, which kind of war?

As American defense analyst Eliot Cohen wrote in reference to Israel,[1] and as I myself have pointed out elsewhere,[2] early twenty-first-century warfare may best be understood by dividing it into three kinds, or parts. The first is the problem of terrorism, guerrilla, and so-called low-intensity warfare waged by non-state organizations either against each other—as in many developing countries around the world—or against states. The second is that of conventional operations, i.e. the kind that are fought by state-owned, regular, uniformed armed forces against each other on the ground while supported by aircraft and, should geography permit, naval vessels. The third is the long-range threat presented by aircraft and surface-to-surface missiles capable of hitting, and perhaps disabling or destroying, a country's military and civilian infrastructure; this also includes the possibility that those missiles and those aircraft will be armed with chemical, biological, or nuclear warheads.

Obviously the three types of war are not entirely separate, but merge into one another. For example, terrorists and guerrillas may one day acquire weapons of mass destruction or, as some experts fear, "mass disruption" (i.e. electronic means with which to disable electricity grids, transportation systems, and other elements of the civilian infrastructure). Far from acting in splendid isolation, they may be, and often are, state-sponsored. Both in the Middle East and elsewhere, some guerrilla groups were simply extensions of the states that supported them; others have deliberately sought to set off sparks that would kindle full-scale interstate war. Whether or not they are armed with weapons of mass destruction, long-range combat aircraft and surface-to-surface missiles may be used, not in isolation but in order to cover and support conventional operations, as both Israel and its enemies have often done in the past. Still, this threefold classification does provide as good a starting point for analysis as is available at present, and I therefore propose to stick to it in spite of all the difficulties.

Considering the global situation as it has developed since 1945, the second kind of war seems to become less important. Numerically it forms a small majority, accounting for fewer than 10 percent of all armed conflicts and continuing to decline all the time. It is limited almost entirely to struggles between, or against, small, weak countries; when it does take place, it tends not to lead to territorial gains and certainly not to such as are recognized by the international community or are followed by peace. No wonder that, with each passing decade, the armed forces earmarked for it are becoming smaller even as the number of weapon systems that those forces possess declines. Take the U.S. as the most powerful state by far. Its armed forces went down from 12 million at the end of World War II to only 1.4 million today; in terms of army divisions the decline was from eighty-nine to ten. Though the air force is often said to be the most future oriented of the services, the 1990s alone cost it 36 percent of its flying platforms.[3] Given the exorbitant cost of modern weapon systems, the day when the entire force only consists of a single aircraft valued at $10 billion may not be as far off as those who first invented the yarn believed. Already, some cost almost one tenth of that; an end to the process does not appear in sight. Just the opposite applies to terrorism and WMDs, whose reach has become global and whose importance is increasing all the time. To realize this fact one need only think of the hole in the ground where, before they were blown away, the Twin Towers used to stand. Or, moving to the other end of the spectrum, count the countries that either already have ballistic missiles in their arsenals or are working to develop them as fast as they can.

Let us examine terrorism and the guerrilla first. From the Israeli perspective, neither is at all new, and indeed one could argue that both were present and had to be dealt with long before the state was formally established in May 1948. Until that date, doing so was mainly the responsibility of the British Mandatory authorities. From time to time they were joined by the Jewish self-defense organization, Hagana. The latter provided a civilian infrastructure, intelligence, and auxiliary personnel. In 1941–1942 some of these personnel also participated in various covert anti-Axis operations, albeit in a very minor way. Among those who had their baptism of fire fighting with the British were Dayan, Allon, and several other future Israeli commanders.

After 1948 the Israeli Army, assisted by the specially created Border Guard, took over. It stood guard and, from time to time, launched punitive expeditions into the neighboring countries from where the "infiltrators," as they were called, came. Both before and after 1948, on the whole these organizations were only moderately successful in their task. Under the British there were three major outbreaks, i.e. 1920–1921, 1929, and 1936–1939. Together they cost the lives of hundreds of Jews and thousands of Arabs; the last one in particular only ended after most of the Arabs' demands had been met. Likewise the IDF, though it was able to reduce the threat, failed to strike at its roots and allowed it to revive from time to time. Nor, given the involvement of other countries in the region, is it easy to see how it could have done any better.

Particularly in the years between 1948 and 1956, the damage terrorists did was considerable, as anywhere between 200 and 300 Israelis were killed and up to 1,000 wounded. So bad was the security situation that the Negev could only be reached in convoy and by daytime; infiltrators got as far as the outskirts of Tel Aviv, and some Jewish settlements in the Jerusalem corridor were on the point of being deserted. The years between 1957 and 1967 were much more peaceful, mainly because King Hussein of Jordan and President Nasser of Egypt did what they could to seal their borders and avoid provoking Israel. However, towards the end of the period, terrorism, now instigated and assisted by Syria's Intelligence Service in particular, reemerged. In both 1956 and 1967, terrorism was one of the factors that helped precipitate the region towards full-scale war, as at least some of those who engaged in it had intended. Nevertheless, compared to the conventional threat presented by the armed forces of the Arab states, the dangers of terrorism were minimal both in 1949–1956 and, even more so, 1957–1967. To that extent, the distinction the Israeli General Staff used to draw between the country's "basic security" and its "current" one was fully justified.

The occupation of the West Bank and the Gaza Strip—that "bone in Israel's throat," as Levi Eshkol once called it[4]—brought large numbers of Palestinian Arabs under Israel's control. Resistance, some of it of a civilian nature but some of it armed, got under way almost immediately; still, on the whole it was muted and ineffective. In part this was because the defeat was totally unexpected and came as a tremendous shock, making every Israeli look as if he were some kind of invincible superman. In part it was because Egyptian and Jordanian rule had been so harsh that the Israeli occupation was experienced by many almost as liberation. For example, King Hussein once used artillery to make the residents of the West Bank pay their taxes; the people of the Gaza Strip had been under night curfew for nineteen years on end. In part it was because the occupied population was swept along in the vast economic upswing that overtook Israel after its victory, which between 1967 and 1973 caused living standards to rise more rapidly than ever before or since. Whatever the causes, twenty years went by before the first *Intifada* started. This was much more than most people (Dayan included)[5] expected, and much more than anyone had the right to expect.

At the time the storm finally broke, those in charge of Israeli policy were Prime Minister Yitzhak Shamir and Minister of Defense Yitzhak Rabin, serving together in a national coalition government. Both were taken totally by surprise; only one day before the start of the Uprising the Israeli Civilian Governor of the West Bank had characterized Israel's rule there as "a brilliant success."[6] Neither was inclined to give way to it and both did what they could to suppress it by force. For over three years—from late 1987 to the spring of 1990—Rabin, to use his own phrase, sent his troops to "break arms and legs." Compared to what other armies, such as the French in Algeria, have done in similar situations the Israeli response was not too brutal. Still it was brutal enough, leading to approximately 1,200 deaths (some of them inflicted by Palestinians on other Palestinians), and many thousands of injured. Tens of thousands saw the inside of Israeli prisons, and the total number of those who did so over the years has been estimated at one-third of the entire adult population.

In the spring of 1990 Rabin resigned. His resignation was the outcome of intrigues in Parliament and had little to do with the Uprising, which was then in full swing and destined to continue under his successor, Moshe Arens. Still, it did put him in a position where he had to rethink his policies. Specifically, in order to form a real alternative to Likud, Rabin and his followers had to turn away from simple repression towards the possibility of peace. The upshot was the 1992 elections and Labor's victory at the polls. Another year passed, negotiations got under way, and the Oslo Agreements were signed. Though many of the details were deliberately avoided, at their core was a promise by Israel's most senior statesmen, Rabin and Peres, that the Palestinians would obtain an independent state at the end of five years. Proving, if proof were needed, that the Israelis' attempt to suppress the Uprising by force had failed.

Whether the Oslo Agreements were doomed to fail, or whether they had a good chance of succeeding but were derailed by actions taken on both sides, will not be debated here. In any case, fail they did. Seven years after the ceremonial signature at the White House, and two years after the final peace should have been signed, there was still no real movement towards an overall political solution in the Middle East. No wonder the Palestinians, with Yasser Arafat at their head, lost patience. First he made sure the September peace conference at Camp David would fail; next, assisted by Sharon who did him a great favor by visiting the Temple Mount and putting the burning fuse to the powder keg, he started the Al Aqsa *Intifada*. In terms of casualties suffered, destruction wrought, and revenue lost, the second Uprising was much worse for Israel than the first. As in the past, ongoing operations by Israel's security forces reduced the number of successful terrorist acts but could not put an end to them. The Palestinians suffered terribly, but never even came close to the point where their will to resist was broken. If anything, the attempts to suppress the Uprising by force have made them even more radical; helping popular support to shift from the secular-minded Palestinian Liberation Organization (PLO) to the more extremist, religiously oriented, Hamas and Islamic Jihad, which emerged as major partners in any political moves. Perhaps the best indication of their determination to triumph or die is reflected by the fact that even Palestinian women have been enlisting as suicide bombers and blowing themselves up. The first time in history this has happened, but definitely not the last.

As Henry Kissinger once put it, guerrillas, so long as they do not lose, win. Israel's failure to prevail is not at all surprising. After all, in 1946–1947 the Jews themselves had engaged in terrorism against their British rulers; some of those who did so are still alive and remember how it was done. While certainly other factors also contributed to the outcome, their efforts ended up by forcing the mighty British Empire to leave the country.[7] From then on, the entire history of post-1945 warfare is one long proof of how hard it is for regular armed forces, specifically including some of the most modern and most powerful ones, to cope with such a threat. Take the example of Chechenya where, according to some, the Russian Army's operations have come close to genocide. Tens of thousands have been killed and many more wounded, captured, or driven from their homes. Yet each time Mr. Putin claims the problem has been brought under control a mighty explosion is certain to tell the world it has not; in fact the Russians only control Chechenya by day, and then only as far as their guns reach.

Israel's own experience in Lebanon confirms the rule. Militarily Lebanon has always been by far the weakest of all Israel's neighbors, with hardly an army to speak of. This, plus the fact that its Christian rulers had at least as much to fear from the growing Moslem population as from the Jews to the south, explains why it never displayed much enthusiasm for participating in the conflict. For twenty years after the 1949 Armistice Agreements the border between the two countries was almost entirely peaceful. Serious trouble only started in the wake of the 1967 War. At that time the Palestinian Liberation Organization obtained a foothold in the refugee camps and began mounting raids across the border as well as launching Katyusha rockets into northern Israel; in 1970, after King Hussein expelled the PLO from Jordan, the importance of Lebanon increased. The outcome was an armed conflict that, with some interruptions, lasted for no fewer than thirty-two years. Israel's first opponent was the PLO. Next it encountered Amal, which in turn was followed by Hizbollah; unlike the first, both the second and the third of these organizations were rooted in the Shi'ite community.

Fourteen years into the struggle, Israel, then under the rule of Begin and Sharon and unable to make headway, decided on a massive invasion of Lebanon. First it mobilized most of its armed forces. Next it overran half the country, inflicted thousands upon thousands of casualties, took thousands more prisoner, forced hundreds of thousands to flee their homes, and brought almost a million Lebanese under its rule. The crowning glory came when it occupied Beirut and stood by as its Christian allies committed large-scale atrocities in the refugee camps of Sabra and Shatilla. The amount of firepower it used was unprecedented in the annals of the Middle East; yet none of these measures stood the slightest chance of showing results. Within two weeks of the beginning of the invasion a vicious guerrilla war got under way. Soon enough, hardly a day passed without vehicles being attacked, buildings blown up, and soldiers killed. In 1985 Israel decided to cut its losses and withdrew to a "security zone" in the south, again to no avail. Having suffered approximately 1,500 casualties in dead alone—proportionally more than the U.S. took in Vietnam—Israel ended up by conceding defeat and withdrawing across the international border in the south.

One peculiarity of the struggle was that the Israelis, specifically including the General Staff, always assumed the worst about their enemies. Vastly exaggerating the power of Hizbollah in particular, they pretended to take seriously its claim that its real goal was to conquer Jerusalem; as a result, time and again they refused to contemplate a withdrawal that might have shortened the agony.[8] Partly for this reason, partly, perhaps, because it sought to safeguard its own standing in society, the IDF appeared determined to hold on at almost any cost. It built mammoth fortifications and filled them with so many arms that, instead of being removed when the time to withdraw came, they had to be blown up. It deployed the best available troops, from the famous *Sayeret Matkal* down, as well as every technological device, from man-detecting radar to attack helicopters, and from rocket-assisted artillery to attack aircraft and missile boats. Some were specifically designed for the purpose. Others, such as a heavy fifty-ton Infantry Fighting Vehicle based on the British Centurion tank, were home-produced and available to no other army on earth.[9] Measure was piled on measure but nothing worked, until, in May 2000, Prime Minister Barak finally threw in the towel.

Thus, Israel's present failure to prevail against Palestinian terrorism merely reflects its own experience and that of others. To some extent, that failure is rooted in the very measures taken to cope with the phenomenon. Take the system under which countless public buildings have been put under guard so that those who enter them are asked questions, passed through metal detectors, have their bodies and belongings searched for weapons, and the like. If everything works as it should, then the result will be the creation of "sterile" zones, as security experts like to call them. As even the most casual visitor can observe, though, in practice the outcome is that queues form as people wait for their turn to be checked. Repeatedly, in the past, those queues themselves have been targeted by suicide bombers. Seeing their entry blocked, all the latter have to do is join one. That was just what happened in the town of Afula on 19 May 2003 when four people lost their lives and others were badly wounded; on other occasions, too, all that "security" achieved was to make sure that some of the victims should wear a badge and a police-style cap. Though a blast at the entrance to a building tends to result in fewer casualties than one that takes place inside, that is scant consolation. Most problematic of all is the fact that the defenses are more suited to keep out the amateur terrorist than the well-trained, well-prepared, professional. Should one of the latter succeed in getting past them, then once inside he will be the only one to possess a weapon and be free to use it as he sees fit; the paradoxes go on and on.

As Israel's own attempts to "seal off" the Territories each time an act of terrorism takes place prove, the one way to solve the problem once and for all is to build a wall. Not a fence, let me hasten to add, but a wall. To prevent people from trying to dig under it, the wall's foundations must be sunk as deep into the earth as the available financial means will allow. Whatever culverts are left to let through rainwater should be blocked by means of grates, and the grates should be fitted with alarm systems. To prevent terrorists from trying to cross it, it must be backed by a death strip perhaps ten meters wide. The strip will be sown with antipersonnel mines and guarded by automatic machine guns. Far from apologizing about the latter, the IDF should make their presence as visible as possible; and, perhaps, advertise it from time to time by firing a couple of bursts into the air. To prevent people on both sides from provoking each other by stationing billboards, making obscene gestures, and the like, an opaque material such as concrete should be used throughout. Briefly, the wall must be made to appear as forbidding as possible and made so tall that, ideally, not even the birds will be able to fly over it. It cannot be high enough, or thick enough, or strong enough.

History shows that walls, provided people are prepared to do what is necessary to defend them and prevent other people from crossing them, by using lethal force if necessary, work. If not for technical reasons— there never has been, nor can be, such a thing as an impregnable wall— then for psychological ones; and if not forever and perfectly, then for long periods and to a very large extent. For example, the Great Wall of China kept out intruders for centuries, allowing civilized life to continue while the barbarians kept baying outside. The same is true of the Roman frontier or *limes;* had it not been for those two immense edifices, history would have taken a different course.

In our own time, an even better example was the Berlin Wall. Particularly between 1958 and 1961, American and Soviet tanks, each with a round in the breach and ready to fire at the slightest provocation, repeatedly faced each other at Checkpoint Charlie. Behind each tank there loomed goodness knows how many intercontinental bombers; all of which were loaded with hydrogen bombs and ready to start. Once the wall had been erected those standoffs came to an end, immediately and almost completely. The reasons were explained to me many years ago by a resident of Berlin who knew his native city well. In part, he said, it was because the wall provided people on each side a secure space within which they were able to breath freely. In part it was because everybody knew exactly how far they could go before being shot and killed; as a result, the vast majority never even tried. Thanks to the much-maligned death strip that ran along the wall such incidents as still took place, particularly those involving people trying to escape from East to West Berlin or accidentally crossing the border (mainly Western children who fell into the canals that formed part of it), were easily contained. Thus a tinderbox that had often threatened to ignite World War III was defused. Eventually West Berlin became one of the most peaceful places on earth, to the point that some people there still look back to the good old days.

Nor does Berlin provide the only modern instance of a wall that works. The heavily fortified fence that separates the two Koreas has been working for fifty years; the one that separates Greek Cypriots from Turkish ones for thirty. The former keeps the peace even though, on paper at any rate, both sides have long refused to recognize one another and have sworn to destroy each other; even today they still trade the occasional machine-gun round. The latter has helped bring relations between the two communities to the point where few people can so much as remember when the last incident took place. In fact, there is even now some talk about pulling it down to allow free passage of people and goods. In April 2003, the first party of Greek Cypriots in decades was permitted to cross the border for a few hours, and used the opportunity in order to visit the places where their former homes had been. Yet few people hate each other more, and have done so for a longer time, than Greeks and Turks. As, given the extensive record of atrocities on both sides (including at least two episodes of large-scale ethnic cleansing, one in 1920 and one in 1974) well they might.

It is true that none of these cases provides an exact parallel; what instance ever does? On the other hand, as of 2004 the fence is working even along Israel's own northern border. Many people regard Hizbollah as one of the more belligerent terrorist organizations on earth. Supported by Syria and Iran, supposedly its members are determined to set the Middle East ablaze, annihilate Israel, blow up as many Westerners as they can, and die a martyr's death if that is what it takes. Even if one does not accept this view, there is no doubt concerning its ability to stir up trouble should it want to. As years of fighting have shown, the organization commands highly motivated, well-trained personnel; if Israeli Intelligence sources may be believed, it has built up a formidable array of rockets capable of reaching to a depth of twenty-five to forty miles inside Israel. Yet in spite of everything, the years since May 2000 have been by far the calmest since 1968, and certainly more so than anybody expected at the time the withdrawal was carried out. As many rounds are now being fired in a month as used to be in a single day; entire weeks go by without the peace of the region being disturbed or anyone being forced to take shelter. What incidents still take place are due almost exclusively to Israeli provocations. No doubt ordered by the powers that be, the air force refuses to recognize that Lebanon is a sovereign country. It routinely violates the latter's airspace in search of intelligence, flying as far north as Tripoli and buzzing the Lebanese coast.[10] Hizbollah responds the only way it can, i.e. by firing antiaircraft guns into the sky; so far, though, not a single Israeli aircraft or helicopter has been seriously hit. As of early 2004, the number of Israeli casualties remains very small. Perhaps the most significant fact of all is that, on both sides of the border but particularly on the Lebanese, tens of thousands of refugees have returned to their homes and are hard at work setting up entire new housing projects. However much their respective governments may bluster, clearly they expect the calm to last.

Even when one limits one's gaze to the Palestinian Uprising, Israel's experience is telling. In 2000–2003 125 suicide bombers crossed from the West Bank into Israel. Of those, a considerable fraction succeeded in achieving their goal, blowing themselves up near their original targets or elsewhere, and presumably joining the seventy virgins who were waiting for them in Heaven. During the same period, as a former deputy chief of staff reminds us,[11] the fence that surrounds Gaza has worked very well indeed. Marked on both sides by a strip of land 200–300 meters wide, equipped with various kinds of ground radar and infrared sensors that feed into a central control room, and constantly patrolled by troops in vehicles and on foot, throughout the Uprising it kept out terrorists almost entirely. It compelled them to confine their operations to Israeli targets inside the Strip—of which, unfortunately, there is no shortage. With hardly any exception, those terrorists who did try to cross were intercepted and either killed or captured. Nor did they succeed in penetrating very far into Israeli territory before meeting their fate; normally it was a question of just a few hundred yards. Among the very few who did get across were two British citizens of Islamic faith who, in late April 2003, used their passports in order to pass through the special gateways reserved for foreigners. One blew himself up in the center of Tel Aviv. The other seems to have been wounded by his own bomb and his body was found later on. Now that this loophole has been discovered, it will be easily closed. Even if doing so causes inconveniences, and even if foreign governments protest.

Already in the spring of 2002, polls showed that almost 50 percent of Israelis were in favor of "unilateral separation," as people here, unwilling to use that terrible word, withdrawal, like to say. Just a year later the figure had risen to over 60 percent;[12] some, dissatisfied with the efforts the government is making (or, rather, not making) on their behalf, have started building fences at their own expense. From former Prime Minister Ehud Barak down,[13] many of the leaders who originally opposed the idea in the name of this or that "national interest" have changed their minds, whereas others were forced to do so whether they wanted or not. There even exists a Political Action Committee, led by one-time National security adviser General (ret.) Uzi Dayan, whose sole goal is to lobby for the wall to be built as soon as possible.

Perhaps an even better indication of the way the wind is blowing is the fact that some of those leaders, however much they may talk about the impossibility of dividing the country and the need to hold on, are perfectly willing to put the taxpayers' money where their mouths are. Had it been up to them then Kochav Yair, the Sharon Valley village where some of the most important among them happen to live, would have been protected by its own wall long ago.[14] In fact, the only thing that prevented *that* particular piece of swinishness from coming about was the public outcry that followed. Yet one would not be surprised to learn that construction is still proceeding in secret or that this section of the wall is given priority; in Israel as elsewhere rank has its privileges and politicians look after themselves first of all. No such protest has attended the erection of similar walls, or fences, around countless other Israeli sites. Starting with the country's only international airport and ending with power plants, fuel and natural gas depots, and settlements located either inside the Occupied Territories or close to them, wherever one goes there are obstacles and more obstacles.

This is where the laws of geometry, or perhaps one should call them Swiss Cheese Avoidance, come in. Not counting over a hundred "footholds," meaning perhaps a few empty sheds or such as hold fewer than ten people, at present there are about one hundred and twenty Israeli settlements dotting the Territories. Before the Israelis reoccupied the main towns in April-May 2002, those Territories were themselves divided into types A, B, and C according to the kind of control they were under. These arrangements have caused the "borders" between Israelis and Palestinians to become so long and convoluted that nobody can keep track of them. To say nothing of frequent changes as settlers establish more "footholds," new roads are opened to link them with each other, Arab towns and villages expand, and the like. The rapidly expanding population makes the West Bank in particular into one of the most dynamic environments on earth; scarcely a week goes by without some change taking place.

Though the terrain is fairly rugged, most of it is passable for men on foot, making it necessary to watch every single inch of the borders in question. Doing so implies maintaining over a hundred more or less permanent roadblocks, while at the same time keeping an eye on the territory that separates them with the aid of surveillance aircraft, patrols, and the like. Perhaps because it is afraid lest public opinion might be appalled by the tremendous waste involved, the IDF does not release data which would allow outsiders to calculate how much trouble and expense it could save by reconfiguring the defenses and combining them into a single, comprehensive, system. One might, however, start by comparing the number of roadblocks that now exist to the number of checkpoints that might be needed in case a wall is built—say four, or five. Next, let us assume that the number of patrols can be reduced in proportion; on that basis, an estimate of up to 80 percent might not be far off the mark.

Let's assume for a moment that such a wall, properly equipped with modern sensing devices—Israel, incidentally, is a leading manufacturer of such devices, which it exports all over the world[15]—and properly watched, is built. In that case, obviously it would be much easier to defend if Israeli forces did not remain on both sides of it; staying put would be the height of folly. To be sure, a withdrawal from the Occupied Territories will not automatically cause Israelis and Palestinians to fall into each other's arms, sign a formal peace treaty, and live together happily ever after. However, it will eliminate what is by far the most important source of friction between them, namely the occupation itself. The daily difficulties, from roadblocks to house searches, that mark the Palestinians' lives will all but disappear; as the poet's saying goes, good fences make good neighbors. The most common forms of terrorism, including knifings, shootings, and bombings (both bombs that are hidden and then detonated *in absentia* and those carried by suicide bombers) will also end almost immediately. So will the kidnappings which, though rare, have taken place from time to time.

To be sure, some of the more exotic forms of terrorism, such as "information warfare" carried by way of the Internet, will still be possible and will have to be guarded against. However, experience so far suggests that the damage they can cause is limited. In any case, they are independent of geography and can be initiated from anywhere in the world. When it comes to attacking web sites and spreading viruses a laptop hooked to a telephone in Buenos Aires is just as good as one in Jericho; in fact it is better. More to the point, the hilly nature of much of the terrain makes it impossible to block the line of sight everywhere. Hence, the Palestinians would still be able to take potshots at Israeli targets, let alone fire mortar shells and rockets across the border. Some may even use shoulder-held antiaircraft missiles to bring down an airliner as it takes off from, or prepares to land at, Lydda Airport. Ways and means to deal with such a contingency are under consideration even now. Perhaps this is one place where the wall should extend further east into Palestinian territory; another possibility would be to protect the aircraft themselves. Still, even if they import far more, and heavier, weapons than they have at present, the Palestinians will have to recognize the fact that Israeli firepower exceeds their own by a thousand to one. Given the almost inconceivably large gap between the economic and industrial power of both sides, there is no reason why Israel should not retain its superiority indefinitely.

Another reason for optimism is because the Palestinians in the West Bank will be geographically isolated. One possibility would be to extend the wall to the Jordan Valley too. The result would be to bottle up the Palestinians, not only from the west but from the east as well; detailed studies of just where such a wall might run are being made even now.[16] Even if this is not done, and the border to the east is left open, the ratio of square miles of Palestinian territory to miles of frontier with Israel will be approximately as seven to one. That is one of the lowest in the world, and only one-third of the twenty-to-one figure which, until 1967, allegedly made Israel "indefensible."[17] Surrounded by Israel on three sides, the only other country with which the Palestinians will have a common border is Jordan. Jordan's Hashemite rulers have as much, or more, reason to fear the Palestinians as Israel does. This explains why the two countries have helped one another control the Palestinians for thirty years and more; exchanging intelligence, patrolling the Jordan Valley, holding meetings in third countries, and so on.[18] As has been the case since at least 1970, the Jordanians will also do what they can to limit the flow of combatants and weapons to the West Bank.

It is, of course, possible that the Hashemite regime will one day be overthrown, either by their own people or by their own people assisted by those on the West Bank. Should the Israelis still be in possession of the Jordan Valley, then there will be no problem. If not, and the two entities are united, then any future Palestinian State that takes up both sides of the Jordan River will still be so outgunned by Israel that a war between them will be no contest. In the air alone, at present the balance is said to be around twenty-five to one;[19] to make things even worse for it, such a State will presumably no longer receive the American financial and technical support that has kept the Kingdom afloat since the late fifties. As to one day replacing that support with Arab aid, experience shows that no Arab state has ever provided more than paltry sums to arm its neighbors. Concerning the Gaza Strip, I have already said that stationing an army in it—assuming it can be done at all—is tantamount to suicide. In all probability, whatever Palestinian leadership emerges in the Territories will join that of Hizbollah in recognizing these facts and keeping things quiet, more or less. If not, then doubtless Israel, freed from the constraints that flow from its responsibility for the population under its rule, will know how to do what has to be done.

What would a wall cost, and how can the benefits it might bring be quantified? Some years ago then Prime Minister Barak appointed a Cabinet Commission to look into that question. It put the bill at $2.5 billion, whereas the most recent published estimate is only about half that figure. How the two sets of data can be reconciled is by no means clear, the more so because the wall now being planned is longer than the original one. Perhaps it is a question of cutting corners by not including the price of the necessary surveillance equipment. Perhaps the different sums named refer to different sections of the wall, or else somebody is deliberately concealing or distorting information; these are problems for the State Comptroller to solve. As to the second question, at peak Israel's GDP was in the order of $110 billion—about $17,000 per capita. During the first two and a half years the Uprising reduced the average living standard by 12 percent and its cost to the economy was estimated at $20 billion. Of this sum, about one third consists of direct military expenses; that includes engineering materials consumed, additional police and Border Guard units established, reservists paid, ammunition expended, equipment worn out, physical damage done, and much more. The greatest indirect losers are tourism and foreign investment. The former accounts for one quarter of all unemployed workers, the latter has shrunk by two thirds, which in turn has compelled the Bank of Israel to maintain insane interest rates in order to avoid a currency collapse. Thus, even if we accept the higher estimate, a wall, supposing it brings the decline to an end, will pay for itself in rather less than a year;[20] surely there are not many investments of which that can be said. The experience of other countries at other times and places, too, suggests that, compared to the cost of waging war, that of a wall will be trivial.[21] Had this not been the case, then presumably they would never have been built, and wars would still be conducted by small groups, hand-to-hand, as, perhaps, they were in Neanderthal times.

Another way of looking at this question is as follows. Early in the 1990s, the Israeli Government approved the construction of a major six-lane highway which will cross the country from south to north, and without which traffic passing through Greater Tel Aviv, the only alternative, was expected to grind to a halt within the foreseeable future. Parts of that road have now been built, and along much of its length they pass within two or three miles of the pre-1967 border. At one point the distance is 350 yards, and at another just 150 yards. As several murderous incidents have shown all too clearly, traffic on Israel's most important artery will only be possible in case a wall is built; this is true regardless of whether the Territories are evacuated. Yet there is no question that, partly because construction is cheaper and partly because much of the necessary land, instead of having to be paid for, is being confiscated from its Palestinian owners without compensation, a wall costs much less than a highway does. Clearly, if enough money is available for the second project then the same is true of the first. The real question is whether Israel can afford to let the multibillion dollar investment in the road go to waste by not building the wall as well.

Once it is established and the Territories on its other side evacuated, the economic impact a wall will have on both sides will be very different. Israel, or rather individual Israelis, will be prevented from importing Palestinian workers except such as will have been selected, screened, and licensed by every means available to the Security Service. In the past, some of those workers have been involved in terrorist acts, either committing them or helping others do so by selecting targets, acting as guides, driving terrorists to their destinations, etc.; hence this will almost certainly represent a blessing in disguise. In fact, Israel's principal problem may well be less to attract Palestinian workers than to get rid of those who, using whatever methods, already live within its territory. Should it want to, it could easily bring in others to take their place. From Thailand through China to the Philippines all the way to the Ukraine and Romania, there are any number of people whose fondest desire is to reach the Promised Land, find work there and, often enough, stay there if they possibly can.

Should the border be as hermetic, and separation as absolute, as it is, say, between Israel and Lebanon, then the former will also lose access to the Palestinian market it now commands. This is a matter of some importance for a number of individual Israeli firms, particularly in the field of light industry, but hardly represents a mortal blow to the economy as a whole. The Palestinians do not have, and probably never will have, the purchasing power to absorb more than a small fraction of Israeli exports.

At the time the Second *Intifada* broke out the figure was below 5 percent. Since then things have become much worse as per capita income in the Territories has gone down by almost one half;[22] as to trade with Jordan and the rest of the Arab world, overt or covert, it is carried out by way of other roads and will remain unaffected.

Though it will take several years, the Palestinians in the Gaza Strip may develop their own deepwater port, permitting them to communicate with the rest of the world without Israeli intervention and control. Not so their brethren in the West Bank; the latter will be cut off both from their main trading partner, Israel, and from the Mediterranean ports. The West Bank economy has long been dependent on agriculture, some light industry, and tourism. All have been badly hit by the *Intifada,* and all will take years before the damage is repaired. Unable to support themselves, its residents will be forced to import everything they need overland by way of Jordan, Syria, and Lebanon. Geography and the absence of good communications make this an extremely expensive proposition as well as an unreliable one (in case those countries' rulers decide to play politics, as they have often done in the past). Alternatively they will have to approach Israel cap in hand to allow them some kind of access to those ports.

To make things easier, one railway might be built to link Haifa to Jenin, whereas another might run from Gaza to the southern edge of the Judean Hills, where its cargo will be transferred to lorries for distribution further north. In both cases distances are short and the country flat. The line from Gaza to Judea might also solve the problem of connecting the two parts of an eventual Palestinian State without exposing Israel to terrorist activity; providing a cheap and effective alternative to the elevated road once envisaged by former Prime Minister Barak. Once they are constructed and are in regular operation, the railways will no doubt increase the incentive of a Palestinian Government to keep its borders as peaceful as possible. If not, then Israel will have some very simple, and very effective, means of retaliation ready at hand.

Those, however, are only the smallest advantages a wall, followed by a withdrawal, will offer in the fight against terrorism. At present, one of the most intractable problems facing Israel is the fact that its own Arab citizens are slowly being radicalized.[23] In part the process is only natural, the result of growing numbers and the self-confidence they generate. In part, it is rooted in the sympathy people feel for their brethren on the other side of the border. From 1967 on, that sympathy has often been reinforced by family ties. Paradoxical as it sounds, the best thing that can happen to any resident of the Territories is to marry an Arab Israeli and obtain the numerous privileges that Israeli citizenship bestows, including the right of residence, the right to work, social security, and, of course, the vote. The recent uproar against a law under which such citizenship is no longer automatically granted merely emphasizes the point.

Some of the radicalization is involuntary, the result of having to deal with, and feeling humiliated by, the daily suspicions which, however understandably, are directed at them at every step. In Israel to look or speak like an Arab is no fun. Doing so can lead to countless forms of minor discrimination; just as holding an ID that marks one's nationality as Arab can lead to some major ones. Another cause is harsh socioeconomic circumstances that the events of 2000–2003 have done nothing to improve. It is true the Israeli-Arab standard of living is much higher than that of most of the neighboring countries; it is also, true, though, that the gap vis-à-vis the Jewish population is growing steadily.[24] Whatever the reasons that underlie it, Israel's own Internal Security Service has often warned the Government that the country's Arabs will not stand by forever, but are being drawn into the conflict.[25] In November 2002 dramatic testimony to this effect was offered by the alleged attempt of an Arab Israeli to hijack an El Al aircraft and smash it into a Tel Aviv skyscraper. In May 2003, it led to half of the leadership of the Islamic Movement being arrested and put on trial. Since then, scarcely a day has passed without incidents, some reported and others not.

Considered from a humanitarian point of view, a wall that separates Israeli Arabs from those in the West Bank and Gaza will be much like the one that used to separate West from East Germany or, what is perhaps the closest parallel, that separates Greek from Turkish Cyprus even now. For some, particularly Arabs on both sides, separation from neighbors and family members will be cruel, a source of suffering and pain. Not so for the vast majority who hate Israel as much as anybody can hate anybody else and who, in day-to-day life, want nothing better than to be left alone and be governed by their own people. For them peace will be tolerable at worst, a blessing at best—each man under his own vine and his own fig tree, as the Bible puts it.

In any case, what such a wall will do is reduce the number of Arabs being governed by Israel by almost three-quarters. The absolute numbers are 4.8 and 1.3 million. Even the last-named number could be reduced if Israel were willing to abandon—as was actually proposed during the Tab Talks of early 2001—some of its prejudices and rid itself of numerous East Jerusalem neighborhoods whose population is exclusively Arab. During the different periods of British and Jordanian rule, villages and suburbs such as Kalandia, Shuafat, and Beth Hanina in the north, and Abu Dis in the southeast, used to be completely independent of Jerusalem. They were only joined to it by the Israeli decision to extend the latter's limits; to this day, their main link with it consists of the municipal taxes to which they are subject and for which they receive almost nothing in return. Certainly there is nothing holy about them, most being little better than overcrowded slums where people live six and more to a room.

As the kidnapping of a taxi driver in July 2003 proved once again, Jews can enter these parts of the city only at the risk of their lives; thus, all a wall will do is to rectify a situation whereby Arabs can go wherever they want whereas Jews can not. The faster the neighborhoods in question are let go, the better also for the Jewish majority in the City as a whole. That majority has been shrinking year by year for the last three decades; during that period, whereas the Jewish population grew 127 percent, the Arab one increased by 204 percent.[26] In this way, letting go is actually a precondition for retaining the rest of Jerusalem. Taking the land west of Jordon as a whole, these measures will cause the number of Arabs under Israeli control to go down from the present 47 percent of the population to 19 percent. That is a much more manageable proposition, and one that may be exercised for a much longer time.

With some luck, moreover, the members of Israel's remaining Arab population will also benefit. As terrorism declines they too will feel safer as they enter a shopping center or board a bus. This is particularly true in the northern and central parts of the country, which is where most of them live and where several have fallen victim to suicide bombers. There will be less chance of them being shot by Israeli police owing to mistaken identity, as happened twice in a single week in July 2003, and the suspicions and harassment that are directed against them will lose some of their sting. Perhaps most important, no longer will they have to watch helplessly as Israel lashes out against their brethren; one can only hope that, as a result, the process of radicalization will be halted or at least slowed down. As is well known, demographic trends are working against Israel. In 1990–2000 the rate of increase for Jews stood at 2.47 percent a year (excluding immigration); meanwhile the Arab-Israeli figure was 3.42 percent.[27] Both for this reason and because the growing participation of Israeli Arabs in the conflict could destroy the country's democracy and terminate the advantages it enjoys in this respect, absolutely nothing is more important than making sure that such radicalization does not develop into a mass phenomenon.

Seen from a military point of view, constructing a wall and getting out of practically the whole of the Territories seems like the only appropriate response capable of putting an end to, and coping with, most, if not all, forms of Palestinian terrorism now and in the foreseeable future. Seen from a military *and* a political point of view such a step, besides removing what is by far the most important motive behind terrorism, is almost certainly the only possible way to de-escalate the conflict. By preventing the Palestinians from coming across the border, marrying Israeli Arabs, and acquiring Israeli citizenship, it will put an end to the "Right of Return" as it is being exercised even now. By preventing Israel's own Arab population from getting involved to an even greater extent than is already the case, it can save Israel from itself. As some Israeli leaders on both sides of the political spectrum have at long last begun to recognize, failure to build it means that Israel will almost certainly be destroyed.

et us assume, then, that a wall already exists. Also, that Israel has withdrawn from the Territories to a border so close to the pre-1967 one as to make any changes strategically insignificant—which, if it is to avoid taking in more than a few thousand Palestinians, would have to be the case. Also, that terrorism is down to negligible or at least manageable proportions as was the case between 1957 and 1967 in particular; a period when, however difficult and exposed the borders, on the average fewer Israelis were killed by hostile action each year than the *weekly* average in 2001–2002. The next question we have to consider is whether Israel will still be able to defend itself against large-scale conventional warfare of the kind that was forced on it by the Arabs in 1973 and which it went out to wage in Lebanon in 1982. In doing this, the changes that have taken place in military technology will have to be taken into account.

First, let's look at the overall balance of forces. As noted above, in both 1973 and 1967 the principal Arab armed forces that fought against Israel outnumbered the latter's army by about two and a half to one. Qualitatively speaking, the equipment used by the two sides was roughly equal. This is not the place to compare weapon systems in detail. Suffice it to say that a different design philosophy often caused individual French, or British, or American-built tanks and combat aircraft used by the Israelis to be more versatile (and more expensive) than their Soviet opposite numbers, combining more capabilities in a single platform. Provided their operators were well trained, they were capable of outfighting their Soviet opposite numbers on a one-to-one basis; the more so because greater attention was often paid to the question of human engineering. By contrast, Soviet weapons were simpler and easier to operate and, in this sense, better suited for the Arab armies whose manpower was often not up to par. They were also developed according to a uniform doctrine and formed part of an integrated system. Consequently they were better at supporting each other and covering the gaps between them. An excellent case in point were the antiaircraft defenses consisting of SA-2, SA-3, SA-6 missiles and radar-directed, quick-firing, ZSU 23-4 cannon deployed along the Suez Canal and on the Golan Heights. Each one was designed to intercept enemy aircraft coming in at a different altitude; together they were formidable indeed, shooting down or damaging almost one quarter of all Israeli combat aircraft before the problem was mastered—to the extent that it was— by movements on the ground. This factor gave the Arabs an advantage that Israel, using many different weapons purchased haphazardly from many different sources, did not possess.

Since then the balance has shifted, almost entirely in Israel's favor. Much of the change is due to the vast economic upswing the latter experienced from the late eighties to the outbreak of the Second Intifada in the autumn of 2000. During that period it was lifted from a semi-developed country into the list of the twenty richest on earth, a ranking which, in spite of all problems, it still retains. In terms of research and development it is a world leader, giving employment to twice as many scientists and engineers per head of population as do the U.S. and Japan.[1] Unprecedented amounts of American and some German financial aid also played a role in enabling Israel to expand its armed forces and modernize them. As even a brief look at the standard international handbooks will show, relative to their enemies those forces are now much stronger than they were at the time they fought their greatest wars and won some of their greatest victories. Indeed, so powerful are they that they almost cause the country to burst at the seams. This is true both on small-scale maps—where signs representing the IDF often take up half the Mediterranean as well—and in some war games where the relevant tokens jostle each other so much as to make them almost unplayable. Nor is the situation on the ground much better. As much as 50 percent of Israel's territory is taken up by the military. Whether in the form of bases, or installations, or training grounds, or land that cannot be fully used for civilian purposes owing to the various things the IDF does, or does not do, with and to it.[2]

Israel's most important weapon systems are F-15 and F-16 attack aircraft, which are controlled by several different kinds of AWACS aircraft. Next in line come Cobra and Apache attack helicopters. The latter are armed with fire-and-forget Hellfire missiles and Forward-Looking Infrared (FLIR) systems that make them suitable for night operations; they are considered particularly important and more of them are being ordered all the time. The ground forces center around Merkava and upgraded Centurion and M-60 tanks (the last-named are in the process of being phased out, and the school that used to train crews for them has been closed). They also have thousands upon thousands of Armored Personnel Carriers, heavy self-propelled artillery with computerized fire controls, and Multiple Launcher Rocket Systems (MRLS); to counter armor they rely on various kinds of antitank guided missiles (ATGWs). The navy, though small, has ultra-modern corvettes and submarines. All three services, but particularly the air force and navy, also have entire families of missiles; some of which, such as the Python IV air-to-air missile, the Popeye air-to-ground missile, and the Barak surface-to-air missile are among the most advanced anywhere.

In point of range, some of Israel's combat aircraft are now capable of carrying several tons of ordnance all the way to Tehran and back without air-to-air refueling (a capability, however, that Israel also has). Many of the weapons are home-manufactured. In fact Israel's ability to design or redesign them and tailor them to its needs is not the least important advantage it enjoys. Compare this with the days when Egyptian tanks, provided by the U.S.S.R. and captured in the Sinai, turned out not even to have appropriate air filters, and, as a result, quickly got stuck in the sand. The same is even more true of the critically important ancillary systems such as radar, avionics, fire controls, night vision equipment, and the like, in all of which Israel is a world leader. All these systems are commanded and coordinated with the aid of the best that one of the world's most highly developed electronics, communications, and computer industries has to offer. Already in 1991, when 80 percent of the ordnance dropped by the Americans on Iraq still consisted of "dumb" iron bombs, the Israeli Air Force no longer had a single such weapon in its inventory; at that time the only UAVs in the U.S. arsenal had been made in Israel. By 2003, too, so good were some Israeli weapons that they were purchased by the Americans for use in the Second Gulf War.[3]

On the other side of the hill the situation is entirely different. Prodded by then General Barak, the Israeli Army began to identify the possibilities of the RMA during the late eighties. Taking appropriate action, in some ways it has pulled ahead not only of many NATO members but even of the United States. This is not true of its Arab counterparts, which for the most part are still stuck with their old, industrial-age weapons and doctrines. To realize how backward they are one only has to compare Israel with the Arab country that has long possessed the most highly developed arms industry, i.e. Egypt. The former exports weapons to dozens of countries from Argentina to Zambia; among the customers are some of the most advanced armed forces on earth. The items sold tend to be on the high-tech end of the spectrum, including everything from electronic warfare gear to ground artillery radar to UAVs of every kind. The latter is content if it can sell off forty-year-old ex-Soviet tanks to Bosnia and send a handful of advisers to train the members of the militias that slaughter each other in the Congo.[4] Needless to say, the situation of other Arab countries is much worse still. Provided they receive foreign technical assistance, as Jordan does, a few of them are capable of introducing limited upgrades to weapons so as to extend their life span. However, not one of them exports arms on any scale, and unless something radical happens chances are that none ever will.

Several factors may explain the Arabs' inability to cope with RMA-type technology. It may have something to do with their rulers' fear of what a networked society, based on the free circulation of information, might do to their dictatorial regimes.[5] In terms of PCs per head of population, Israel enjoys an advantage of 30:1 and 1,000:1 over Egypt and Syria respectively.[6] Some Arab rulers deliberately limit Internet access by exercising control over it and making it much more expensive than it need be. With a population of 275 million the entire Arab World combined only uses twice as many mobile telephones as Israelis do,[7] which in turn is both cause and consequence of the fact that they have hardly any electronic industries. There are no real Arab equivalents to IAI, Elbit, Elsint, Elop, and the rest. Even in the age of globalization, one cannot always buy everything off the shelf. Even if one does, integrating many kinds of hardware into a functioning system is a supremely difficult task. Doing so requires a large computer-literate population from which future experts can be selected and bred. Though some of the programming work may be left to foreign mercenaries, differences in language and outlook may result in a true Tower of Babylon at the time the system is installed and, perhaps even more so, when the time for upgrading comes. In view of the spread of "information warfare," such an approach may also not be without problems when it comes to maintaining security. To paraphrase a well-known proverb: One army's security expert may easily become another army's hacker.

Looking beyond the military sphere, technological backwardness is both cause and consequence of the fact that the gap between the Arab countries' per capita GDP and that of Israel has been widening steadily over the last fifty years. At present, in the cases of Syria, Jordan, and Egypt, the figure is anywhere between 6 and 8 percent—which in turn translates into 3 to 4 percent of the American per capita GDP. Even Saudi Arabia's fabulous oil reserves only give it a per capita GDP about half of Israel's.[8] Instead of leading to development, the reserves in question have produced addiction. The outcome is a backward and fanatical society whose political stability has long been in some doubt; while it does possess the outward trappings, in some ways it is not a state at all. Should the present regime disintegrate, then the absence of a strong civil society may cause the country to revert to the gathering of warring tribes it used to be until the 1930s. Such poor countries may put their armed forces on parade, as North Korea also does, making an impression on TV watchers who do not realize what the smart turnout really amounts, or does not amount, to. However, they do not modern armies build.

As far as numbers, equipment, and organization are concerned, by far the most powerful Arab force remains the Egyptian one. Like Israel, Egypt receives American military aid. However, the sums in question are smaller by about one-third; nor can Cairo command additional U.S. aid in the form of massive subsidies that Washington extends to Israeli Research and Development projects such as the Arrow antiballistic missile, a laser system for shooting down Katyusha rockets, and others. As in the case of Israel, American money can only be spent in the U.S. for buying American equipment. This has enabled the Egyptian Air Force to substitute F-16s for MIG-21s—a great leap forward—and its army to put M-60 and Abrams tanks in place of the old T-55s and T-62s. The navy with its modern missile frigates and submarines is also strong. Favorably situated, geographically speaking, of the three Egyptian armed services it probably poses the greatest danger, threatening to cut Israel's sea-lanes or bombard the coast as it has tried to do in the past. On the other hand, the very aid that has enabled Cairo to build up its armed forces also constitutes that army's Achilles' heel as, no doubt, it was intended to be. Suppose the worst happens and Egypt, either under the present regime or a different one, decides to violate the Camp David Agreements and start preparing to fight Israel in earnest. In that case presumably Washington will not hesitate to pull the purse strings, leaving its client high but not at all dry.

At the operational level, perhaps the decisive fact is that the enormous, integrated air-defense system that played such a large role in shaping the October 1973 War no longer exists. Most of the antiaircraft missiles that Egypt still retains date to the 1960s and 1970s. Among them are Soviet-built SA-2s, SA-3s, and SA-6s (the same that proved ineffective against NATO aircraft during the Kosovo campaign); there are also some upgraded American Hawks, and some French-made Crotales. The only really modern element consists of American Avengers, however, those are light missiles unlikely to make an impression on anything but low-flying aircraft and helicopters; in any case, Israeli helicopters have been carrying antimissile defenses for years. Briefly, Egypt is exposed to the tender mercies of the much stronger Israel Air Force and some put the difference in offensive power at almost two to one.[9] In particular, should the Egyptian armed forces try to reoccupy the wide-open spaces of the Sinai, then the number of surface-to-air missiles needed to protect them will be astronomical and the forces' vulnerability will grow in proportion. Such a move will also get them out of their fortifications and extend their lines of communication. Left open to precisely the kind of armored maneuver warfare that has long been the IDF's specialty,[10] they are quite likely to end up as the Iraqis did in the Kuwaiti Desert in 1991.

As past experience shows only too clearly, the Arab armies' ability to make an impression on Israel has always depended on them attacking, or at least engaging, their enemy on more than one front. This is why the fact that, on Israel's northern border, the Syrians have lost much of the punch that almost enabled them to overrun the Golan Heights back in 1973 is critically important. In part, Syria's eclipse as a military power is due to the fact that Turkey has formed an alliance with Israel. Ankara is breathing down Bashir Assad's neck, threatening to cut off his water supply and even invade his country should he go too far in supporting the Kurds. Israeli pilots have been training in Turkey for years, and it is not inconceivable that, under some circumstances, they will be permitted to fly operational missions as well. Thus, even before the 2003 Gulf War added to its worries by leading to an expanded America military presence, Syria was threatened by a two-front conflict against the two strongest military powers in the Middle East.[11] Certainly such a war is a possibility that Syrian planners cannot afford to ignore. In the words of Vice President Abd al-Halim Khaddam: it is "the greatest threat to the Arabs [read, Syria] since 1948."[12]

As late as 1985–7 the Syrian Army, having suffered heavy losses in Lebanon, was still trying to achieve what Assad Sr. called "strategic parity" with Israel, buying massive numbers of armored vehicles and artillery barrels and setting up several new divisions.[13] However, since then it has deteriorated to the point where most of its equipment consists of old junk. For example, the T-72 tank, the most modern one in the Syrian inventory, was defeated by Israel's Merkavas as far back as 1982. Yet since then the latter has gone through three more versions that have enhanced its capabilities several times over; in the Gulf in 1991, American Abrams tanks blew off the turrets of Iraqi T-72s as if they were toys. The last time the Syrian Air Force sent its aircraft to fly sorties against the Israeli one the results were a hundred to one in the latter's favor. No antiaircraft missile in the Syrian arsenal was purchased later than 1986. As in the case of Egypt, some date back to the October 1973 War. Unlike those of Egypt, they have not been upgraded since; overall, the difference in offensive power between the two air forces is put at five to one.[14] The last naval engagement, which Israel also won hands down, likewise took place in 1973. Since then the Syrian Navy has been reduced to three unserviceable submarines, a handful of 1960s-vintage missile boats, and a few light craft. It cannot even look the Israeli Navy in the face; yet without a naval opponent the Israelis will be free to bombard the Syrian coast as they have done in the past.

In part, Syria's weakness is the result of age-old internal factors such as its dictatorial regime, which in the past sometimes forced it to keep the best units in reserve so as to guard Damascus against a coup. Another reason is the low quality of the manpower at its disposal; mainly, though, it originates in the fact that the Soviet Union, which for twenty-something years after 1967 provided Syria with twenty-six billion dollars' worth of weapons at prices Damascus could afford, has itself disintegrated.[15] So long as the age of "industrial" warfare lasted the U.S.S.R. was able to keep its military hardware up to world standards, more or less, producing very large numbers of comparatively cheap and simple, but nevertheless well-designed and effective, systems. However, the onset of the RMA and the new role played by high tech has caused the relative quality of that hardware to deteriorate; as the twentieth century gave way to the twenty-first it was often no longer competitive. Some countries that rely on Soviet materiel even turned to Israel to upgrade it for them, enabling the latter to earn foreign currency by designing and installing new avionics in old fighters and new guns and fire controls in old tanks. Even when they do have weapons to sell, Russia's new rulers differ from their Soviet predecessors in that they will only do so at world prices and for hard cash.[16] Cash is something Syria, whose citizens' per capita GDP went down by 10 percent between 1996 and 2000, is very unlikely to obtain in the foreseeable future. In fact the two sides are still haggling over equipment Damascus purchased during the second half of the 1980s and has yet to pay for.

As a result of all these factors, in one year alone (1996) Israeli arms imports exceeded those of Syria by thirty to one, no less.[17] In the next year Syria's purchasing power fell so low that it took the trouble to buy 200 antiquated T-55 tanks in the hope of upgrading them; yet only a hero or a fool would approach an Israeli Merkava in one of those. Apart from some surface-to-surface missiles, chemical weapons, and ammunition, Damascus has no answer to Israel's indigenous military production. Now that the Americans control Iraq, Syria, having lost the billion or so dollars per year Saddam Hussein used to pay for permitting oil to flow from the production centers at Kirkuk to the Mediterranean ports, has become poorer still. No wonder that, to quote a former head of Israeli military intelligence (spring 2003), Syria is "not a threat" to Israel.[18] It is said that, to compensate for his weakness in real life, Bashir Assad likes to play the kind of computer games in which he can shoot down aircraft and bust tanks.

When Iraq is added to the equation, the shift in Israel's favor appears much greater still. More than any other Arab country Iraq combines, or used to combine, vast oil wealth with a considerable and relatively well-educated population. Hence it has long had the potential to become one of Israel's most powerful adversaries in spite of the distance—400 miles or so of uninterrupted desert—that separates the two countries. Its various regimes have been so hostile to Israel that the two countries have never even signed a cease-fire; during the first decades of Israel's existence Iraq participated in every one of the Arab wars against it except the one of 1956.[19] As far back as 1948, Iraqi troops were among the most dangerous of all. Israel at that time did not yet have an air force capable of attacking the Iraqis while they were still east of the Jordan River. This enabled the enemy to come within ten miles of the Mediterranean; one of those who received his baptism by fire fighting against them, and who never forgot the experience, was Ariel Sharon.[20] Having been repulsed on this sector of the front the Iraqi forces regrouped and threatened Israel's main communication line to the north, Wadi Ara, from which they had to be dislodged by force of arms. In 1967 their successors again made their way towards the Jordan River, only to be stopped by the Israeli Air Force, which also attacked some of Iraq's own air force bases. On each occasion the Iraqi involvement grew and grew until, in October 1973, a 60,000-strong expeditionary force was sent to Syria's aid. Partly because they started too late, partly because of obstacles the Israelis put in their way, only one or two brigades actually arrived on time and participated in combat. Being unfamiliar with the terrain, the Iraqis turned out to be bad soldiers and were repulsed without difficulty. Still, they did help bring the Israeli advance on Damascus to a halt.[21]

As Egypt gradually moved towards peace with Israel during the second half of the 1970s, Israeli generals and policy makers sometimes talked of Syria, Jordan, and Iraq as forming an "Eastern Front." On paper the "Front" appeared formidable. It had at its disposal as many troops and major weapon systems as did all NATO's European members combined; including 1,000 combat aircraft, 200 combat helicopters, 7,000 tanks, 1,500 high-quality APCs, almost 3,000 artillery barrels, and 800,000 to 900,000 men.[22] In practice its rulers were divided, what with Baghdad accusing Damascus of being too soft on Israel (Syria had accepted U.N. Resolutions 224 and 328) and the latter retaliating by calling the former "right wing" and "fascist." The third member of the trio, King Hussein, feared his would-be Arab partners as much as, or even more than, he did Jerusalem, and with very good reason. Regarding Hussein and his dynasty as illegitimate and as traitors to the Arab cause, the Syrians had often tried to topple him, or assassinate him, or embroil him with Israel by sending terrorists through Jordanian territory. The Iraqis on their part sometimes tried to turn Jordan into a protectorate or else use it as a staging ground against Israel from which they could operate without undue risk to themselves. Hence the chances of the king joining another military adventure against Israel were not great.[23] In September 1973 he even went so far as to meet with Ms. Meir again and warn her of the impending Egyptian-Syrian offensive, though neither she nor Washington, which received the same warning by intelligence channels, listened to him.[24]

Perhaps more ominous was the fact that Iraq had long acted as a kind of strategic reserve on which Syria, in particular, could draw. This was all the more so because the weaponry and doctrines of the two armies were supplied mainly by the Soviet Union and were quite similar, making cooperation easier. Through much of the 1970s; Iraq used its vast oil revenues to build up the largest armed forces ever seen in the

Middle East. When the time came, though, Saddam Hussein, who had taken over in 1979, did not turn them on Israel. Instead he launched a murderous eight-year war against Iran. He thus made certain that the "Eastern Front" would remain a mirage, causing Israel to heave a sigh of relief; at one point the IDF's then chief of staff, General Refael Eytan, expressed the hope that the two sides would fight each other forever.

In 1988, the victorious conclusion of that war marked the high tide of Iraqi power. At peak, Saddam commanded about 700 combat aircraft, one million troops, 5,000 tanks, and armored personnel carriers and artillery to match. He also had about 1,000 surface-to-surface missiles, some of which had been purchased from the U.S.S.R. and North Korea whereas others were home-manufactured. Though badly made and extremely inaccurate, some of the missiles had the range to reach Israel, and some were apparently capable of carrying weapons of mass destruction that Iraq also had. Once again Saddam, instead of directing his forces against Israel as his self-imposed mission as a later day Saladin would have required, used them against another Arab country and invaded Kuwait. The upshot was the 1991 Gulf War, in which Iraq was badly defeated. Between equipment destroyed and that which, after ten years of sanctions, was no longer operable, that War probably cost Iraq about two-thirds of its military might, including, though that was unknown at the time, whatever "strategic" missiles and weapons of mass destruction (WMDs) survived the United Nations inspections. The little that remained was immobilized by Anglo-American airpower; when the Second Gulf War came in 2003, the Iraqis barely got a single aircraft off the ground.

Whether, following Iraq's second defeat and occupation, the Americans will succeed in rebuilding the country and providing it with a more or less stable, more or less pro-Western, government remains to be seen. If they do, then the danger to Israel will be gone; such a government will have its hands full rebuilding the country and defending against Iran. If, as seems more likely at present, they do not, and Iraq turns into a Middle Eastern version of Afghanistan, then it will also be gone. Another possible outcome is that the country will be broken up as both the northern and southern provinces drop away. Protected by the Americans and infiltrated by the Turks, the former have been largely self-governing from 1991 on; in the future they will set up their own Kurdish State and become embroiled with the Arab south in a dispute over borders (including the great oil fields of Kirkuk) and revenues. The latter are Shiite strongholds that have tried to break away in the past and may not want to stay under the rule of the Sunnis from central Iraq. One way or another, as a military power Iraq has ceased to exist. An American failure to establish control may enable terrorists to use the country as a base, but it will take a very long time before it is rebuilt and regains its political freedom of action. Even if it is rebuilt and does achieve that freedom, given the geographical distance that separates it from Israel, any threat it poses will be limited to missiles and weapons of mass destruction; on which, more below.

The conventional armed forces of Jordan and Lebanon are too small, and those of Iran too far away, to carry much weight. The last-named ones are sometimes said to present a threat to Israel, and in fact one may easily envisage a scenario whereby Iran will emerge as the main beneficiary of Operation Iraqi Freedom. Such a development, however, is many years in the future. For the present, the Iranian armed forces only amount to one-third to one-half of the Iraqi ones at their peak.[25] In 1997–2000 alone falling oil prices and economic mismanagement caused Iran's per capita GDP to decline by one-third, from $1,500 to just over $1,000 a year;[26] hence they are unlikely to be reinforced in the near future. Nor does Iran have what it takes to launch an RMA, any more than the Arab countries do.[27] While Iran does have some military industries, their quality can be judged from the fact that it has only found customers in Bosnia, Lebanon, Libya, and the Sudan. However much the ayatollahs may dislike Israel, they are sufficiently intelligent to allocate what money they have to spend on conventional arms, building up their naval forces so as to protect their lifeline in the Gulf, not on an army capable of reaching Jerusalem. Had anyone thought of launching such a campaign, it would have been ruled out by logistic considerations alone. The days when light cavalry could emerge out of the steppe and roam where it would, firing arrows and feeding on local resources, are long gone.

Thus, at least as far as the balance of conventional forces goes, and at least on paper, Israel's military advantage over its combined adversaries is much greater than it was in either 1973 or 1967.[28] One might, indeed, argue that, for the first time in its fifty-year history, the country no longer faces a conventional threat at all; nor are the leaders on the other side ignorant of these facts. Take Egypt's President Mubarak, himself a former air force commander in chief. In May 2002 he considered it necessary to warn his more hot-headed countrymen that starting a war against Israel is not a good idea;[29] what a change from the time when his predecessor, Sadat, stated his determination to recover the Sinai even if it cost Egypt a million men. Though this was certainly not what he meant, the same applied when Bashir Assad said that Syria would be in danger as long as Israel continues to exist. By any conventional standard that may be applied, the balance of forces between the two is just too lopsided.

Should Israel return to its original borders, more or less, then once again its most important problem will consist of its lack of strategic depth. Once again, an enemy stationed in the West Bank will occupy the high ground, making it necessary to think about how to resist an offensive into the coastal plain and cope with any reinforcements that may try to make their way westward across the Jordan River. Once again most of Israel's vital points, greater Tel Aviv and Jerusalem specifically included, will be exposed not only to an armored advance but to rockets and artillery fire. Practically all of these difficulties will result from surrendering control of the West Bank to the Palestinians. By contrast, and certainly as long as the Sinai remains demilitarized, an Israeli withdrawal from the Gaza Strip will only affect the conventional balance of forces to a very small extent, if at all. In other words, the Strip is irrelevant to the problem at hand; if necessary it could be reoccupied in a couple of hours and any forces that it contains demolished. For that reason it will not be discussed further.

Suppose such a withdrawal takes place; Israel's first problem will be to gain intelligence concerning a possible attack from the east. At present such intelligence, as well as early warning, is provided by whole arrays of sophisticated antennae positioned on the mountains that mark the north-south watershed, as well as hills along the Jordan Valley. As these assets are lost, it will be necessary to find another solution. The one that comes to mind is balloons or, to use a more technical-sounding term, aerostats. Over the last few years aerostats have been of considerable interest to many armed forces, which see in them a possible way for carrying heavy loads over difficult terrain;[30] compared to conventional aircraft their advantage is that they are cheap to run. As anyone who has driven around in the western Negev knows, the Israelis are even now using them to look across the Sinai and detect any Egyptian attempt to remilitarize it. Something similar could be deployed opposite the West Bank.

To be sure, owing to the difference in topographical height—the high ground, remember, will be in Palestinian hands—the balloons in question will probably have to be of a different type. Some, particularly those flying over Jerusalem, may be tethered, but others may have to be precision-steered along the border by means of small turbo-prop engines. Others still will fly out over the Mediterranean, well away from any antiaircraft missiles that may be aimed at them. As a rule of thumb, the closer to the border they fly, the more capable balloons are of maintaining line-of-sight contact with the areas under surveillance, an important consideration for gathering certain kinds of intelligence. On the other hand, the higher they fly the further into enemy territory they will be able to look. The main challenge will be to make sure that observation is carried out continuously and is not interrupted by any kind of weather.

At present, the most important balloon-developing centers are Germany, the U.S. and Japan. Some of those under construction have a speed of eighty knots per hour. They can stay aloft for two weeks on end, and are capable of carrying a payload weighing as much as twenty or thirty tons. Others are meant for service at altitudes up to 70,000 feet and, if all goes well, should be able to operate nonstop for as long as ten years.[31] Partly because Israel is a small country, partly because its designers are seldom carried away by gigantism as foreign ones sometimes are, requirements could probably be much more modest, and expense much smaller. Performance would fall somewhere in between; say, a few thousand pounds carried to a few thousand feet for a period measured in weeks until maintenance becomes necessary and a replacement is sent up.

In principle, one type of payload could consist of equipment similar to that carried by the American Joint Target Attack Radar System (JSTARS) aircraft for monitoring the movements of both hostile aircraft and ground troops; indeed this is one field where Israeli firms are already cooperating with American ones.[32] Another would be look-down radar to intercept low-flying aircraft and cruise missiles. In addition to headquarters, the data gathered will be relayed straight to the batteries of Patriot antiaircraft missiles deployed further east, providing them with a few minutes' worth of additional early warning and helping to enhance their performance. Once again the U.S. Army is already experimenting in this direction. Experience shows that where America leads, Israel is seldom far behind; sometimes, indeed, the sequence is reversed.

As the performance of sensors continues to improve, and as computers and data-links continue to be miniaturized, a fairly small number of balloons—perhaps four or five—should be capable of carrying aloft all the intelligence apparatus Israel needs. Compared with present ground-mounted systems, the main shortcoming of balloons will be their extreme vulnerability even to light antiaircraft artillery, which is cheap and easily available. Yet too much should not be made of this fact. In case any of them is fired at or shot down, then of course this, in itself, will provide the best available early warning; in view of this fact, it might make sense to have some of them act as decoys and carry potatoes instead of antennae. As long as replacements are readily available the loss of a balloon will present no great problem, particularly if it were unmanned, whereas the sensitive equipment it carries could be made to self-destruct, either automatically or upon an order being transmitted from the ground. Finally, compared with conventional aircraft, balloons have the advantage that their power plants are much smaller—a fact, incidentally, that makes them less vulnerable to infrared-guided missiles—and that their airframes do not have to cope with great stress. As a result, on a per-hour-of-flight basis they are far cheaper and easier to maintain.

Next, defense proper. The most important plan for defending Israel without the West Bank was presented by General (ret.) Israel Tal.[33] Tal first gained his spurs as a commander of the armored corps and a divisional commander in 1967. He served as deputy chief of staff during the difficult months immediately following the 1973 War, fathered the Merkava tank, and several times received the Israel Prize for various defense-related R&D projects. He is thus as well qualified as any expert in Israel and abroad; at one point, indeed, he had his portrait placed in the American Armored Commanders' Hall of Fame. The background to his proposal was formed by the fact that, at a time when Israel was governed by Ehud Barak, peace and the establishment of a Palestinian State in much of the Territories appeared within reach. To that extent, it may reflect the former prime minister's own thought, though the two had their differences in other respects. Tal's ideas were supported by the commander in chief of the navy, General Yedidya Ya'ari.[34] Both men developed a suggestion first raised, albeit only as a joke, by Ezer Weizman.[35] While none of the three went into detail, all proposed that, to compensate for the coming loss of strategic depth, Israel would have to create artificial depth by beefing up its naval forces. The problem may be divided into two parts, conventional and unconventional. The first will be dealt with now, whereas the second we shall postpone until the next part of this study.

As is well known, the decade since the 1991 Gulf War has been overshadowed by what the Americans like to call the Revolution in Military Affairs.[36] As the events of 9-11, as well as Israel's own experience in Lebanon and the Occupied Territories, demonstrate, the revolution in question will probably be of limited help in combating terrorism, much of which takes place under the "technology threshold," so to speak. On the other hand, its impact on conventional interstate warfare is expected to be, indeed already is, revolutionary. One historical analogy that comes to mind is the invention and integration of the arquebus—the first effective handheld firearm—which between about 1525 and 1600 helped the *tercios* to sweep all in front of them and Spain to become the most powerful state on earth. An even better one is the construction by Guderian and others of the Panzer divisions, an innovation which, during the 1930s, made the Wehrmacht into the most modern force on earth; and which, by 1941, enabled it to come within a hair of winning the Second World War.

Adapted to Israel's needs,[37] the heart of the system could consist of an ultrasophisticated network of sensors, electronic communications, and data-processing systems. Instead of being separated by unit or arm of service, as has hitherto normally been the case, all could be integrated with each other in what one expert calls "a system of systems." All could hopefully act as force multipliers, scanning the theater of war, locating and identifying targets, tracking them, establishing priorities among them, and designating them for the kill. Some of the mountains of data generated by the system may, perhaps, be processed automatically—in fact, developing the necessary software is perhaps *the* greatest challenge facing the designers. The rest will be displayed on arrays of consoles and used by headquarters at all levels in order to command and control the army's fighting "teeth." In addition to manned aircraft, those teeth will consist of Unmanned Combat Aerial Vehicles (UCAVs) and smaller UAVs. In the more remote future, one may also think of the kind of long-range, sea-borne artillery being developed both in the U.S. and Europe.[38]

Most of the new flying platforms are considerably smaller, cheaper, and easier to build and maintain than conventional aircraft, with their expensive, highly vulnerable, life-sustaining systems. Another advantage is that the necessary operators do not have to actually pilot them in order to gain experience but may be trained largely by using simulators. Even as purchasing prices rise as new capabilities are added, this factor will cause wear and tear to be reduced; over the lifetime of the system, the savings are expected to be in the order of 65–75 percent.[39] While operating UCAVs does require both training and expertise, they do not need the same kind of high-quality personnel as manned aircraft do, a consideration that is not unimportant in a small country where such personnel are always scarce. Finally, should one of them be shot down or lost, it will be unnecessary to have an entire organization standing by to save the pilot, which is not only expensive but also endangers other pilots.

Some of the new systems will no doubt have to be stationed aboard specially constructed warships. That, however, is an extremely expensive proposition. Warships tend to be crammed with crew, machinery, and whatever gear they require for their own self-defense. Hence, what space they can provide for sea-to-ground operations is usually limited; the same is even more true of submarines that some experts, with the U.S. in mind, have proposed for the purpose.[40] Take a typical modern U.S. aircraft carrier. With their dead weight varying from 80,000 to 90,000 tons, they are the largest fighting machines ever built, a triumph of engineering design. Yet the surprising thing about these modern-day Behemoths is that every single inch of space is fully occupied. As a result they can only launch about thirty-five attack aircraft out of a total of ninety or so; the rest consist of self-defense interceptors, antisubmarine craft, and a variety of aircraft and helicopters used for electronic warfare, liaison, and logistics. Backing up those thirty-five—usually considered sufficient to generate about seventy sorties a day—requires no fewer than 5,000 crewmembers, 300 pilots, and entire flotillas of escorts and resupply ships. Since America is the world's sole remaining superpower, and since it also happens to be a global island, its desire to "project" power without having to depend on allies is understandable. Still, so long as the carriers only use conventional weapons, the ratio between teeth and tail is, to say the least, extraordinary. The more so because, to remain out of reach from land-based aircraft and surface-to-sea missiles, they tend to stay out of narrow seas, thus extending the range and causing the number of daily strikes they can deliver to decline further still. Had Winston Churchill been alive today, he might have said that never did so many bucks generate such a small bang. The total cost, including also those of suitable bases, repair facilities, and the like, will easily run into tens of billions of dollars, thus putting it beyond the reach not just of Israel but of practically all other countries, too.

To save money, it may prove practical to put most of the above-mentioned devices aboard different kinds of ships altogether. The objective must be to maximize deck space on which to base weapons. One solution would be to buy an old aircraft carrier and modify it. Although their strategic situation is entirely different, both India and Thailand have taken this path; surely if they can do it, so can Israel with its incomparably superior military-industrial resources. A second solution would be to resort to specially constructed catamarans, which, lying low in the water, have the additional advantage that they are hard to detect. A third solution, which in the short run at any rate might be the most feasible of all, would be to use modified container-type ships so as to exploit the large cargo-carrying capacity they offer. Whatever ships are finally selected, they will be defended against attack partly by sea-to-sea and sea-to-air missiles, partly by "soft" defenses such as chaff, electronic countermeasures, and decoys,[41] and partly by an escort consisting of warships, which, incidentally, already carry similar defenses. In addition it may be feasible to protect the container ships by having them mix with ordinary commercial traffic, of which the Mediterranean has plenty.[42]

While the existing literature has emphasized the possibilities of naval vessels, they do not provide the only possible basing mode. Compared to conventional aircraft UCAVs, let alone missiles, cruise missiles, and UAVs, are small, mobile, and hard to locate and hit.[43] Not having pilots, UCAVs can withstand G forces much higher than manned aircraft can. It should therefore be possible to launch them with the aid of disposable rocket boosters and use cables or nets to retrieve them when they come down to land; the necessary technology is readily available both in Israel and abroad. The others can be, in fact already are, launched from many kinds of ground vehicles, from modified trucks up. As technology advances, it may even be possible to launch some UAVs from cruise missiles and UCAVs, thus providing them with an independent intelligence-gathering capability. Whatever the precise solution, the bases all these devices require will be incomparably smaller, less expensive, and less vulnerable than present-day airfields with their extensive runways, superexpensive underground maintenance facilities, prominent control installations, and, often enough, entire housing projects. All this will solve, or at least greatly reduce, what may be the most important single problem that an Israeli withdrawal from the Territories would create, namely, the proximity of its air bases to the country's borders.

How well developed are existing devices of this kind, and what are the kinds of mission they can be expected to accomplish? To answer these questions, let's start by looking at cruise missiles. Disregarding the World War II German V-l, as well as several other experimental contraptions developed (but never deployed on any scale) during the 1950s and 1960s, the first cruise missiles were introduced by the U.S.A. during the 1970s.[44] The original intention was to use them as stand-off weapons for delivering nuclear warheads from the air, extending the life of the strategic bomber force which, following the 1973 Arab-Israeli War, was seen as being threatened by increasingly effective ground-to-air defenses. Later, owing to the usual interservice rivalry, other models were developed capable of being launched from the land and sea as well. The end of the Cold War left them without a mission, causing them to be modified for carrying conventional payloads, too. Originally they were so expensive that only the superpowers could afford them, a factor that often caused their use to be regarded as grossly wasteful. By now, however, technological progress has caused their price to drop so much that small, simple ones are within the reach of many countries.[45] Some of the necessary technology is akin to that used in sea-to-sea missiles and spreading rapidly; both China and Iran, neither of whom is known for their sophisticated military industries, have produced them and put them on display. Recently it has even been suggested that anyone with the necessary know-how and $10,000 in the bank could build one in his own garage,[46] though just how far the missile could fly, how accurate it would be, and what payload it could carry is not clear.

Originating in the period before the invention of the microchip, the early cruise missiles were guided by a specially developed Terrain-Contour Following Radar (TERCOM). Not only was it extremely expensive to build, but the missiles had to be locked on their targets before being launched. Recently, however, things have changed as they were provided a Global Positioning System (GPS). This means that cruise missiles are, or soon will be, capable of being redirected in mid-flight in response to rapidly changing intelligence;[47] the result will be both to save money and to provide the kind of operational flexibility that is at the heart of the RMA. The usual high-explosive warhead apart, payloads might consist of cluster-type ammunition. Another more exotic possibility currently being studied would be to equip them with directed-energy weapons.[48] Doing so would fit them for use against various sensors, radar, communications, and computer systems, briefly anything that contains (or will soon contain) a microchip; leaving out, as has been said, only knives, sticks, and stones.

Compared to cruise missiles, the chief advantage of UCAVs is that they are retrievable and reemployable. Already, some UCAVs under development in the U.S. have a 10-hour loitering time at 250-mile range and a maximum range of 750 miles, which, given the geography of the Middle East, is more than enough to intercept any ground forces preparing to attack Israel. Future ones will be capable of staying aloft for several days. They will constitute a constant threat that will have to be reckoned with at all times. They would limit an army's movements, compelling it to take measures in self-defense, and perhaps creating psychological difficulties for its troops who, aware of the flying menace, will never know when it is about to strike. At least one, the American-built Predator, is operational. It has been tested both in Afghanistan and in the 2003 war against Iraq, where one or two were shot down. Originally designed as a platform for surveillance, reconnaissance, and electronic warfare, reportedly the Predator has also been employed to take out individual Al Qaeda terrorists driving a car in Yemen.[49] If it and the Hellfire missiles it carries are accurate enough to do this, then clearly they are accurate enough to do almost anything; apparently the difficulties which, even a few years ago, prevented their use against mobile targets are on their way to being solved or have been solved.[50] In the future, perhaps the principal challenge will be to increase their payload so as to enable them to carry more than one missile per mission. Like cruise missiles, moreover, UCAVs may one day be modified to carry directed-energy weapons. The possibilities appear limitless.

Having been among the first to enter the field, the Israelis' ideas on UCAVs parallel American ones in some ways and differ from them in others.[51] The Americans already have an operational UCAV capable of firing a missile at ground targets. Compared with the Americans, the Israelis have an easier job to do: they neither need nor favor large, high-altitude, very long range, costly machines such as the suitably named Global Hawk. First, they are expensive; second, the Middle East is not sufficiently large to provide scope for them. More than the Americans, they have started thinking about how to prevent UCAVs from being shot down as several were during the 1999 Kosovo and 2003 Iraq campaigns. One possibility would be to provide them with electronic defenses against surface-to-air and air-to-air missiles. In the past, such defenses have been quite effective in protecting manned aircraft. Hence there is no reason why they cannot be made to do the same for unmanned ones as well.

The commander of Israel's Air Force, General Dan Halutz, says he can even now foresee the day when manned air surveillance and reconnaissance will have become a distant memory. The same source expects the next stage in unmanned air combat to consist of platforms dedicated to attacks on airfields and air-defense suppression; already, part of the second task may be entrusted to an unmanned version of the old F-4 Phantom fighter-bomber. It is true that Halutz and others expect manned air-to-air combat to be around for several decades yet. On the other hand, with so many unmanned platforms flying about and performing various functions, clearly its role will diminish and one might well ask what such combat will still be needed for.

Unlike UCAVs, UAVs are not designed for participating in combat but only carry intelligence payloads. Compared with cruise missiles and UCAVs they have the advantage that they are smaller. Present-day ones can weigh as much as a quarter of a ton and their normal wingspan is between nine and twelve feet. In the future, miniaturized electronics and a decrease in the amount of power they need for their operation may permit that wingspan to be reduced to one foot or even less. This means that some UAVs may themselves be capable of being launched either from UCAVs or cruise missiles;[52] yet another possibility would be to base them on helicopters. Payloads either being carried at present or under development include tiny TV cameras, other sensors such as infrared and magnetic, and data-links that will enable them to communicate with satellites as well as ground control stations. Much in the way that navies have long used various decoys to simulate the movements of ships and submarines and protect them against sonar, moreover, it is conceivable that UAVs will be used to simulate the movements of larger flying platforms. This will enable them to mislead and confuse the defense; once again, the possibilities appear limitless.

Whatever the precise technologies employed, they should permit Israel's security border to remain where it is, i.e. in the Jordan Valley. As it has long done in reference to the Straits of Tiran, Israel will make it very clear that an enemy attempt to cross the river in force will constitute a casus belli.[53] As long as the current regime in Jordan continues to exist, there should be no problem. Should this situation change one day, or should Jordan be united with Palestine, or should somebody else try to cross the country from east to west, then hostile preparations will be detected well in advance with the aid of equipment carried by the above-mentioned balloons. In case a decision to launch a strike is made, AWACS aircraft—Israel, incidentally, already has some of the most sophisticated ones now in existence—will take off. They will supplement the balloons and take over from them if necessary. Perhaps, to minimize the threat from surface-to-air missiles, they will fly out over the sea. Given Israel's small size, they can do so without an appreciable decrease in their effectiveness. Even at present, a single reconnaissance pod carried by a single EC-8 aircraft, operating at 30–150 miles distance from the area under surveillance, is capable of covering 20,000 square miles per hour of flight.[54] Other systems, including such as are carried by Israel's F-16 attack aircraft and old F-4 Phantom fighter-bombers, are also capable of locating ground targets, even at night;[55] in this as in some other respects, when it comes to electronic warfare small does not necessarily mean worse. The primary purpose of the data generated by these platforms will be to give the IDF's UAVs their marching orders. Swarms of them will take off, loiter over the battlefield, identify the enemy's formations, track them by means of laser designators, mark targets, and send the information back to headquarters where it will be fused in something very near to real time.[56]

Economically and technically, the difficulty of building modern armed forces is extraordinary. Developed countries far larger, richer, and technologically more advanced than the eventual Palestinian State only get a very small return for their investment. Having spent billions, perhaps more, often they end up with a handful of air force squadrons and even fewer major ground formations to match. Looking through the handbooks, one is reminded of the Emperor of Lilliput and the armaments he prepared against Belfuscu; had it not been for massive U.S. aid, then of course Israel itself would scarcely have escaped this fate. Should Palestine become independent tomorrow, then its GDP will be around $4 billion. Assuming 10 percent of this is spent for security purposes, a very high figure by international standards (though not by those of the Middle East), then per capita military expenditure will be $100 annually compared to $1,700 in Israel. The Government will find that, in the entire West Bank (let alone the Gaza Strip), there is no room for a first-class air base, and certainly not one that would be beyond the reach of the IDF's heavy artillery. For these reasons, any regular army the Palestinians may one day be able to field will consist almost solely of light units—some infantry brigades, perhaps, with few if any heavy weapons and even fewer of the complex electronic networks needed to coordinate them.

In a way, indeed, by constructing such forces, building bases for them, and then deploying them, the Palestinians would be doing the IDF a favor. Notoriously, one of the most difficult aspects in any guerrilla campaign is deciding on the right moment to switch from the so-called second stage to the third, involving open warfare. In 1968, at Hue and Khe San, and in 1972 along the Demilitarized Zone, Hanoi made that decision prematurely, causing its troops to leave cover and launch conventional offensives. This in turn permitted the effective use of artillery and B-52 bombers to target the attackers, leading to slaughter on such a scale as to almost stagger the imagination.

Since 2000, something similar has been taking place on Israel's northern border. Now that Hizbollah is building bunkers and deploying rockets, gathering intelligence about it has become much easier.[57] It also presents a much better target than it did when its members still operated in the terrorist mode. If worst comes to worst, the entire area could once again be overrun and the terrorist infrastructure demolished in short order—forty-eight hours or less. Hizbollah's own leaders are well aware of these facts. That is one reason why they procured long-range rockets; the outcome is a conventional balance of terror that has enforced peace. Similarly, the regular forces of a future Palestinian State, whatever they may look like, should be small enough to be handled by IDF ground and air forces, even without mobilization. This is all the more the case because the RMA is tilting the balance towards the defense. An Israeli ground strike may not be necessary at all, firepower alone being enough to hit the enemy so hard as to render him incapable of further operations.

What applies to the Palestinians will also apply to any non-Palestinian Arab forces trying to approach from the east. They too will be discovered well ahead of time. If they fail to stop, then the next step will be to subject them to a hail of missiles and UCAVs—a strategy known as "putting fire into the enemy's territory." Perhaps the bombardment will start while they are still trying to descend from the Trans-Jordanian plateau into the Valley below; certainly by the time they mass to cross the Jordan River in order to make for the hills to the west. In a way, doing all this will represent no more than pouring new wine into old bottles. With few exceptions, Israel's strategy has always been to target the enemy's armed forces rather than his population, his economic infrastructure, his leadership, or whatever. This doctrine has served it well in the past, and will be applicable to the future, too.

In this context, two facts are particularly relevant. First, in the event of a withdrawal, the most vulnerable part of the Jordan Valley, (the open country that leads west from Beth Shean towards Esdraelon) will remain in Israeli hands as it was before 1967. Second, and as has already been pointed out, any force that runs the gauntlet and succeeds in entering the West Bank opposite Samaria and Judea will be vulnerable to being cut off by an Israeli pincer movement. Compared to 1967, its work will be made much easier by the fact that there is now a first-class road running the Jordan Valley's entire length. Assuming the columns move at fifteen miles an hour, the entire operation will only take about four hours to carry out; preparing for it, perhaps Israel should be well advised to widen the part of the road that runs along the western shore of the Dead Sea. As the Arab columns make their way west, so rugged is the terrain that they will be limited to three or four axes. Should they try to leave those axes then the few vehicles that make it will be left without rear services and without supplies; should they stick to them, they will be set up for the kill. Once again, the events of June 1967 provide a perfect precedent. On the second day of the War the Sixtieth Jordanian Armored Brigade, which until then had been held in reserve, was sent to join the fight. As it tried to climb the road from Jericho to Jerusalem, it was caught by the Israeli Air Force and annihilated. Its blackened remains used to litter both sides of the road for years; a grim warning to anybody who might try to do the same again.

The military burden of facing the Syrian Army is not inconsiderable and forces Israel to maintain a small armored division on the Golan Heights at all times. Still, compared to the West Bank and Gaza Strip, the great advantage of the Golan is that there is hardly any non-Jewish civilian population to speak of. With no terrorists to combat, life on the Heights is actually safer than it is in the center of Tel Aviv; few people there can even remember when the last shooting or bombing took place. Socially speaking the cost of holding on to the area is trivial.

In part, this is because there are no holy sites to worry about, pilgrims to escort and protect, international complications to be avoided, etc.. Partly it is because the Golan is geographically remote and never formed part of the Land of Israel, even in its pre-1948 borders, and partly because there are only 20,000 Jewish settlers whose political leverage is minimal. In any case, the occupation does not give rise to the kind of impassioned controversy that swirls around Gaza and the West Bank. To the contrary, even many left-wing Israelis who would like nothing better than to hobnob with the Palestinians see Syria as an implacable and barbaric enemy. The dislike, which has something irrational about it, is often justified by pointing to the days when captured IDF soldiers were badly mistreated; today, too, Bashir Assad is made to carry part of the blame for the fact that Hizbollah does not release any information about Israeli prisoners it holds. Whatever the origin of the sentiment, it tends to unite Israelis in a way that other issues do not. If necessary the Golan can be held indefinitely, or else until peace comes.

At present a treaty with Syria that could lead to an Israeli withdrawal from those Heights seems unlikely. Hence this volume does not deal primarily with what a post-withdrawal defense might look like; still, a few thoughts about that problem are in order. The most prominent, and militarily most important, terrain features on the Golan Heights are a number of hills such as Mt. Hermon, "Booster," and a few others. Like those along the Jordan Valley, they are festooned with IDF intelligence-gathering sensors that provide a direct line of sight towards Damascus, presumably picking up each Syrian aircraft as it takes off and each Syrian armored battalion as it moves from one place to another. As in the case of the West Bank, a combination of balloons, UAVs, and AWACS aircraft might well form an acceptable alternative to those sensors. Overflying the terrain, and properly coordinated, they might, indeed, be preferable; the reason being that the latter two in particular will be much harder to locate and destroy by artillery fire or surface-to-surface missiles.

Intelligence apart, perhaps the most important consideration is that the southern part of the Golan Heights, in particular, is open, flat, and largely devoid of topographical obstacles, in many ways constituting ideal tank country. Taking this fact into account, in 1973 the Syrians launched a simultaneous attack all along the forty-eight-mile-wide front, inundated most of the defenses, and left them behind; a maneuver that, during the first two days, almost cost Israel its control over the area. Suppose, however, Israel withdraws from the Heights to the Valley below. Again, as in the case of the West Bank, the attacking columns will be have to be force-fed into one of the five—in reality, since the one on the extreme south is practically useless, four—roads that lead down from the Heights. Since most of the terrain on both sides is impassable, they will have great difficulty either leaving those roads or coming to each other's aid.

It is true that the distance that separates the Golan Heights from the pre-1967 border is much smaller than that between the Jordan River and Israel, giving the latter almost no time to react. On the other hand, the Upper Jordan Valley differs from the Plain of Sharon—downhill from the West Bank—in that it scarcely represents Israel's heartland. A successful Syrian offensive against that area might lead to one or two kibbutzim being overrun, as also happened during the 1948 War; that, incidentally, is the origin of many of the difficulties concerning the fate of these areas that have bedeviled all attempts to negotiate peace. It would not, however, put the country's existence at risk. To do that, it would have to penetrate much further in the direction of the Valley of Esdraelon and Haifa. But that is a completely different proposition; and, as long as Israel retains its overall military superiority in the air and on the ground, hardly a realistic one. Tactically speaking, an Israeli ground force that tries to counter a Syrian attack by climbing the slopes will be at a great disadvantage (although, as the 1967 War proved, not necessarily so great as to make the operation impossible). Equally obvious, conventional artillery firing from the Valley will also be at a great disadvantage.

Suppose, however, the Israelis take up the possibilities that the RMA provides—or, since this has already been done to some extent, adapt them to the problem at hand. The first step would be to reconstruct the early-warning and intelligence-gathering system. The one that emerges must be capable of detecting enemy preparations continuously, by day and by night, and in every kind of weather. It should also be robust, meaning that it cannot be simply destroyed or interrupted by enemy action. In addition to the above-listed balloons and aircraft it might include permanent warning stations on the eastern slopes of the mountains of Galilee. Those mountains are, after all, as tall as the Golan Heights themselves. With the exception of two roads that cross them from east to west, they are also quite as difficult to ascend. The fact that the new stations will be further away will also make them harder to hit and destroy; an advantage which, in some respects, recommends their construction even now.

It has been argued that, compared to the stations now mounted on the Golan Heights, future ones located in Galilee will be unable to look behind the hills, Mount Hermon in particular, allowing the Syrians to avoid detection by concentrating some forces behind them. Given the state of present technology, that is true enough; indeed, an argument over this question and how to resolve it was one of the key factors that prevented Israelis and Syrians from coming to an agreement in the past.[58] Still, not too much should be made of this factor. The largest hill, and the only one that really presents a problem, is Mount Hermon. Still, even its size is limited, and so is the size of the army formations it can provide with cover. Any Syrian attempt to "disappear" units from the order of battle by using the mountain for maneuver and deployment will itself provide a warning that something suspicious is afoot, causing the IDF to be put on alert. Besides, Israel already has a satellite capable of discovering such units and tracking their movements, albeit not continuously or as frequently as it would like. Should additional satellites be launched in the future, they may help alleviate that problem, too.

Imitating the security arrangements in the Sinai, one possibility would be to divide the Golan into a partly demilitarized eastern zone and a completely demilitarized western one.[59] Other possibilities would include similar security arrangements on Israeli territory (as Syria demands), border adjustments, and the stationing of international forces. The number of possible trade-offs is endless; taking a leaf from the Cold War, the American mediators at various points suggested the installation of "hot lines," mutual advance notification concerning military maneuvers, and much more.[60] One retired Israeli general who, probably acting on Rabin's instructions, has studied the problem in some detail believes that demilitarization should be able to provide the IDF with twelve to twenty-four hours advance warning against an impending attack.[61] As aircraft are brought to a state of readiness, artillery and tactical surface-to-surface missiles pushed forward to within striking range, vehicles refueled and loaded with ammunition, and so on, their movements will scarcely escape notice. As was also the case in 1973, the main problem will be less to detect preparations—at that time, every single Syrian unit was correctly identified—than to ensure the enemy's intentions are understood; and, once understood, acted upon.

The alarm having been sounded and the decision to go to war made, the system should switch to marking the enemy units' precise location and tracking their operations. Given the size and vulnerability of the intelligence-gathering stations, it must be assumed that at least some of them will be knocked out. This would be the moment to activate the flying platforms and, with them, an entire new generation of ground sensors. Such sensors are now under development both in the U.S., which has deployed them in Afghanistan and in many other countries. Deployed from the air, inside specially developed canisters, once they hit the ground they are supposed to right themselves, extend their antennae, and activate their systems. Some can detect the noise made by passing motor vehicles. Others pick up the ground vibrations that the same vehicles generate, whereas others still rely on infrared radiation and disturbances of the magnetic field to do their work. All, of course, will be provided with tiny wireless datalinks. Where they will differ from their predecessors of an earlier generation is that they will communicate with each other, comparing "signatures," filtering them, and triangulating them. As the task of friend/ foe identification (FFI) will be entrusted to special transponders carried by friendly forces, the final outcome should be a digital map of the battlefield. That, in turn, will permit headquarters to be fed with a constant stream of data. The enemy's precise location, direction of movement, speed, etc. will all be noted. Perhaps the time will even come when some of the decisions as to which targets to prioritize and which ones to leave until later can be made automatically by suitably programmed computers; as, after all, is already the case in many forms of antiaircraft and antimissile warfare.[62]

Next, the Israeli Army should discard many of its tanks and artillery pieces. In the case of the former this is because their guns do not have the requisite range and are, in any case, ill-suited to firing uphill. In the case of the latter it is because they are insufficiently accurate to hit moving targets; although, supposing that problem is corrected by adding so-called "brilliant" munitions, their lives may be extended. The job of taking care of heliborne operations—the Syrian Army still retains the powerful commando forces that played a prominent, though hardly decisive, part in the 1973 War—will be divided between the IDF's ground troops and its air force. The former will use Stinger and Redeye shoulder-fired antiaircraft missiles which, back in 1973, they did not have; the latter will have some of its attack aircraft standing by for the purpose at all times. Other aircraft will strike at the enemy's rear echelons, if absolutely necessary by flying in from the south as they did in 1973.

To take care of advancing enemy tanks the Israeli Army should build its first line of defenses around its missile-firing attack helicopters. It is true that such helicopters are fairly vulnerable to ground fire, as was proved once again by the Americans in Iraq; unlike the latter, though, the Israeli ones will only have a short distance to fly and will do so over friendly territory. Their task will be to shoot up the last tank in the column, the first one, and, that having been accomplished, everything in between as well. Finally, to take care of soft targets accompanying the tanks or operating independently of them, the IDF will rely primarily on high-trajectory, precision-guided missiles dispensing cluster-type ammunition. In this context it is interesting to note that Israel, cooperating with Romania, has been developing a large-caliber, long-range version of the Multiple Rocket Launcher System in its arsenal.[63] Doing so makes excellent sense. The longer the range, the greater the space in which it will be possible to disperse the weapon-carrying vehicles and maneuver them, and allowing them to move from one firing position to the next, making them hard to find, and rendering them immune to counter-action.

Shortly before he was assassinated in 1995, Prime Minister Rabin came within a hair of concluding an agreement that would have led to Israel's withdrawal from almost all the Territories captured by Israel from Syria as a result of the 1967 War.[64] Attempts to make the Israel Defense Force release information, either about the thought it devoted to the possibility of defending the country in case Damascus broke the agreement and resumed hostilities or concerning the conclusions it reached, have not yielded any results.[65] Compared to the prime ministers who came after him, Barak included, Rabin was more interested in peace and more prepared to make concessions; hence the repeated Syrian demand that the talks be resumed from the point where he left off. Even so it is inconceivable that he did not have his subordinates, including two successive chiefs of staff, Generals Barak and Shachak, who participated in the talks, consider the problem and solve it to his own satisfaction. "Mr. Security," as he was known during his mature years, was the most methodical of men. In 1948, as a twenty-six-year-old brigadier, he had seen at first hand what lack of proper preparation can cost an army. Since then, by his own testimony,[66] he was determined to make sure that, in the future, Israel would never again have to enter a conflict under such conditions. During his term as chief of staff (1964–1967), he was constantly preoccupied with Syria, proving that he was as mistrustful of it as anybody else in Jerusalem and, perhaps, even more so than was really necessary under the circumstances. Thinking of what a force equipped with weapons such as have just been described, properly coordinated and commanded, may do to an invader, one can only repeat the words Dante saw engraved on the gates of hell: Abandon all hope, you who enter here.

Whereas, at least until the 1973 War inclusive, the greatest challenge facing Israel was the one posed by the ground forces of its Arab neighbors, since 1980 or so that situation has been changing. As we saw, Israel's drive to develop a nuclear program originated during the early years of the State. On Ben Gurion's initiative a Nuclear Energy Commission was established and scientists were sent to prospect for natural uranium; later a small reactor, useful for scientific and training purposes, was constructed at Nahal Shorek. Just when the leaders of other Middle Eastern countries learned of the program's existence is not clear. At the latest, this must have happened in December 1960, when pictures of the Dimona Reactor, then under construction, were leaked by the CIA and published in the London *Daily Express;* forcing those leaders to do, or at least pretend to do, something whether they wanted to or not. Not long afterwards the much-publicized launching of an experimental Israeli ballistic missile known as the Shavit told the Arabs that their enemy was also working on delivery vehicles to match.

Over time, the Arab leaders' reactions to this situation have been mixed. Some demanded, in vain, that Israel halt its program, and indeed the Arabs' suggestion that the Middle East be turned into a nuclear-free zone has long been a bone of contention between them and Jerusalem.[1] Others—among them Egypt's president, Gamal Abdul Nasser—threatened action, including preventive military action. The more time passes and as more American documents are declassified, the clearer it becomes that the desire to do something about the emerging Israeli nuclear threat was one factor in the complex train of events that ended in the outbreak of the June 1967 War.[2] Perhaps, in closing the Straits of Tiran to Israeli shipping, what Nasser really wanted to do was to bargain for the Dimona Reactor to be put under international inspection; this, after all, was not unlike what Kennedy did to Russia over Cuba only five years earlier. Others tried to persuade Israel's Western patrons to do something to halt the Israeli program but, on the whole, did not succeed in their aim as those patrons either looked away or claimed they were in no position to act. Others still used that program in order to justify their own policies. Be they strident but useless speeches; or a tacit move towards nonbelligerency; or a turn towards guerrilla warfare; or anything else.[3]

During the 1960s several of the leaders in question also started developing weapons of mass destruction; chemical, biological, and nuclear.[4] In the past Israel's own leaders have been paranoid about those developments, and with very good reason. Time and again they did whatever they could to obstruct them. They contacted the home states of the scientists who ran the programs asking for help; threatened the scientists themselves with assassination; and actually helped a few of those who did not listen meet their maker in the next world. Israeli agents also sabotaged the components of one Iraqi reactor before they could be shipped, whereas the Israeli Air Force launched a preventive strike that left another one in ruins. Official circles in Jerusalem sometimes refer to such a strike as the "Tamuz Option," providing more than a hint that a repetition cannot be ruled out. Still, the fact is that only a few of these programs were launched in response to the Israeli threat or are primarily directed at Israel. To present the entire Arab, let alone Islamic, world as if it were bent on nothing but the earliest possible destruction of Israel is simply false. Even if it *were* true, it would still be useful to distinguish between the parts of that world which are actively working to achieve that aim and those whose only contribution to the cause consists of rhetoric; focusing to counter the former and doing no more than watch the latter.

Let us start our *tour d'horizon* with Egypt, the Arab country with the largest population and the greatest potential for producing military power. Egypt's per capita GDP is very low and it is not exactly one of the world's most developed industrial nations. On the other hand, an even lower GDP has not prevented other, even less developed, countries from acquiring the bomb; if Pakistanis could "eat grass" (former Prime Minister Zulfikar Ali Bhutto) to finance their nuclear program, so presumably could Egyptians. Unlike some other Arab countries, both richer and poorer, Egypt does have a fairly large, well-educated, well-trained, technical and scientific elite, as well as the universities and technical institutes capable of turning out the necessary personnel. Had Cairo really focused its resources on the matter then it could have launched a nuclear program in the 1970s and, probably, built its nuclear weapon at some time during the 1980s. Possibly this would have been done with foreign assistance of the kind that Canada has provided to India, France to Iraq, and Russia to China and Iran;[5] not to mention the aid Israel itself received from France. In any event, Egypt has refrained from taking this road, though whether it did so for ecological and economic reasons (as was claimed at the time),[6] or because it did not want to get into the way of its new American patrons (as seems more likely) is not clear.

Ever since the Camp David Agreements were signed over twenty years ago, the Government of Egypt has done whatever it could to preserve the peace with Israel. On the other hand, the period also saw a steady, if uneven, deterioration in the relationship between the two peoples. No wonder the Egyptian masses, watching first Israel's invasion of Lebanon and then the measures it took to put down two successive *Intifadas*, did not like what they saw; by now, if anything the government is less anti-Israeli than the people are, and is holding the latter in check. Whoever is to blame, the outcome has been a very "cold" peace indeed. At present Egyptian strategy, including large-scale attempts to settle the

Sinai Peninsula, is clearly defensive. However, a scenario where the two countries may find themselves at war again cannot be entirely ruled out. This is especially true in case the Israeli-Palestinian conflict is allowed to drag on and to escalate; what happened back in 1948 may happen again.[7] Whatever else, such a scenario would place Egypt in a markedly inferior position in respect to both conventional and unconventional weapons.

The upshot of these considerations has been a large and well-developed chemical weapons program capable of producing several kinds of blister gas, asphyxiating gasses, and nerve gasses. Published sources are coy about these programs and fail to say that Egypt has actually produced those weapons, and for very good reason; had evidence to the contrary been available, then it would immediately produce conflict with the United States. On the other hand, Cairo has refused to adhere to the international convention against chemical weapons so long as Israel does not sign the nuclear nonproliferation treaty.[8] It must therefore be assumed that it has them and/or is capable of producing them in short order. The necessary delivery vehicles in the forms of Scud missiles produced in cooperation with North Korea are also available.

As noted above, Syria has long been one of Israel's most bitter enemies and this case is indeed characterized by an irrational element that is absent from the relationship between Israel and many other Arab countries. Unlike Egypt, Syria also has a territorial conflict with Israel over the Golan Heights, which it is determined to recover by means fair or foul; any Syrian Government that openly renounces that objective will probably not last. Yet its conventional armed forces are no match for the Israeli ones, the more so because they can no longer count on Egyptian assistance to split the enemy. In the past there has often been talk of Damascus acquiring a research reactor, but so far lack of financial means has prevented it from taking even this preliminary step towards a nuclear program; besides, Syria does not have the necessary human infrastructure as Egypt does. The solution was to turn towards chemical and biological weapons that are much easier to develop and build. The program gave it an offensive option which may be exercised at some future time, although the Syrians must know that the IDF will respond tenfold and that doing so is tantamount to suicide. More likely, the weapons' primary purpose is to act as a deterrent in case some Israeli minister of defense, acting with or without his Government's consent, decides to launch another unprovoked attack on Syria as happened in 1982 and, the way Damascus at any rate sees it, in 1967 too.[9] To this must be added the fact that Syria also has Turkey and, until recently, Iraq to think about. The former is both strong and, owing to the Kurdish problem and a long-standing territorial dispute, a dangerous rival. The latter, though it usually stood by Damascus against Israel, always had the potential to become the stronger of the two.

Next, consider Iraq. At least since 1958, when the monarchy was overthrown and a military regime substituted, Iraq has sought to play a leading role in the Arab world by presenting as radical a face as it could. As in the case of any would-be Arab "leader," its ability to do so depended partly on devising ways and means to "confront" Israel. Paradoxically, the fact that the two countries do not share a common border helped. It provided Baghdad with some room for maneuver and allowed it to play at brinkmanship without having to fear the consequences as much as other Arab states did. In case war did break out Iraq would not have to fear an Israeli invasion of its own territory; at worst, part of the expeditionary force it had sent would be destroyed.

For the same reason, Israel only represented a secondary threat to Iraq, whose most immediate headaches were its neighbors, Turkey and Iran. Of the two, the former sits across Iraq's main river, can cut off its water supply whenever it chooses to, and, in the past, has threatened to do so. With the latter it shares a long and hotly disputed border along the Shatt al Arab River and elsewhere. The populations of both Iraq and Iran are predominantly Shi'ite. Nevertheless, relations between them have often been hostile, causing them to look at one another with suspicion and hatred. People on both sides use the word by which the other is known as a term of abuse; and both governments have intermittently done what they could to destabilize the other by playing the Kurdish card. Yet, in the end, Iran is three times as large as Iraq. By some accounts it also has "imperial" pretensions dating back to a time when not only Mesopotamia but the entire Middle East as far as the Bosporus was ruled from Ktesiphon. In short, Iraq's rulers would have had very good reason to think about WMDs even if Israel had never existed. At some points during the 1980–88 Iran-Iraq War, indeed, such weapons were almost the only factor that saved them from destruction.[10]

While Iran no longer borders on the Soviet Union, it still has Turkey and, until recently, Iraq to think about. What is more, in the form of Pakistan, its neighbor to the southeast, Iran also has a nuclear-armed neighbor right on its own doorstep. It is true that relations between the two countries have been amicable on the whole. Still, there have been occasional bones of contention. A fairly recent one was Pakistani support for the Afghan Taliban which, Tehran feared, could lead to its own eastern provinces being destabilized. Should the Taliban return to Kabul one day, as does not seem impossible,[11] then this and other issues might be reopened, putting Tehran in an inferior position. Much worse for Iran, beginning in the spring of 2003 it has been surrounded by American forces from no fewer than three directions, i.e. south (the Persian Gulf), east, and west. To say nothing of Washington's budding alliances with, and military presence in, Iran's northeastern neighbors Kazakhstan, Kyrgyzstan, and Uzbekistan.

The way U.S. military technology works, for every nonnuclear artillery round and missile in the arsenal there is usually a nuclear version as well. Hence any American forces, anywhere, must be assumed to be nuclear-capable as a matter of course; those that are not so at present can easily be made so by adding a few aircraft or missiles. Remembering what happened to Saddam Hussein, who was attacked and destroyed for no very good reason, some would say that, if ever a country had good reason to go nuclear as fast as it could, it was Iran in 2003. This is all the more so because the Bush Administration takes to the words "Islamic Republic" as a bull takes to a red cloth. It has often made threats against Tehran, and Defense Department officials have explicitly refused to rule out the option of waging war against Iran.[12]

Whatever the rationale behind them, all the programs do affect Israel in one way or another. To be on the safe side, Jerusalem must consider capabilities as well as intentions and look at them as if they *could be* directed at it one day. This even applies to Pakistan. Pakistan's overriding security concern has always been its Indian neighbor. No Pakistani government has ever threatened war against Israel, and if New Delhi may be believed there were times when the two countries conspired against it. Islamabad does not have missiles capable of hitting Israel and is not expected to acquire them in the near future. Yet Pakistan is also an underdeveloped Islamic country with an ideology to match. As any amount of propaganda and occasional acts of terrorism against Western targets make clear, radical currents are always just under the surface. Israel is decidedly unpopular, and never more so since it has begun to develop a strategic relationship with India in the 1990s. When President Musharraf, prodded by Britain and the U.S., suggested that Islamabad might recognize Israel, the domestic reaction was so violent as to force him to drop the issue like a hot potato;[13] worst of all, the regime is notoriously unstable. Should it come to resemble the one in Tehran, or should the country disintegrate as Afghanistan did, then a danger might well develop.

To sum up, as of late 2003 Iraq is no longer in the picture and may be disregarded for years, perhaps decades, to come. However, Syria, Egypt (which, in the 1960s, used gas to combat tribesmen in Yemen), and Iran (ditto, during the War against Iraq) all either have chemical weapons or are able to produce them quickly.[14] Iran is also said to have a massive nuclear weapons program that is expected to bear fruit between 2005 and 2008,[15] albeit that such predictions have now been floating about for over a decade and, so far, have always been disappointed.[16]

Launching an RMA takes tremendous amounts of money and expertise. Not so acquiring or developing delivery vehicles for WMDs, which is much cheaper and easier by comparison. All of the necessary technology was already available to the Germans in 1944–1945; at a pinch, it will still do service today. Several of the above-mentioned countries have long possessed attack aircraft capable of reaching Israel and this still remains the case today. In the face of the Israeli Air Force's undisputed command of the sky, the likelihood of a hostile aircraft getting through the defensive umbrella is relatively small. Still, since it is WMDs we are talking about, even a single successful sortie might inflict enormous damage; as a former Egyptian chief of staff once put it in the crudest possible way, how many nuclear bombs can Israel absorb? Ignoring Iraq as irrelevant for the present, countries that already have surface-to-surface missiles include Egypt, Syria, Saudi Arabia, and Iran.[17] There has also been talk about dispensing chemical and biological weapons by some more esoteric means, such as cruise missiles and UCAVs, although, at present, no Middle Eastern country has made great strides in acquiring or developing them. In short, even now Israel is faced with delivery systems capable of carrying WMDs and of being launched at it by several different opponents from several different directions. At least one country, Syria, also has enough deployed surface-to-surface missiles—the number is estimated at 260 or so—to deliver them to almost every point from the northern border down to the Gulf of Eilat. Therefore, no account of Israel's defense can be complete without considering that threat.

How, then, will a withdrawal from the Territories affect Israel's ability to cope with the threat just outlined? As the prophet of airpower, Giulio Douhet was one of the first to point out,[18] compared to those that take place on land and at sea, the great advantage of air operations is that they are largely independent of geography, and also of topographical obstacles of every kind. Ground armies will always have to take into account the existence of mountains, forests, rivers, lakes, marshes, roads, and, above all, the towns and villages whose people can either provide assistance, as in making resources available, or engage in resistance. Seas and oceans are free of topographical obstacles and also of human inhabitants, providing navies with greater freedom of action; however, maritime operations are still constrained by the existence of obstacles such as shallow coasts, islands, and, above all, straits. All these will enable them to base themselves on certain shores but not on others. They will be canalized into certain areas, seas, or oceans, compelled to ignore or bypass others, and find their maneuvers either facilitated or impeded; both the speed of movement and the directions it can take will be affected. Traditionally technological limitations meant that the inland reach of navies was limited to cannon range. Armies on their part were entirely unable to operate at sea; of these considerations, the second remains in force today. By contrast, aircraft will operate over both land and sea, crossing and recrossing the shoreline without any difficulty. They will also fly right over every kind of terrain or obstacle without their speed, or modus operandi, being influenced in any way. The same is even more true of missiles, either ballistic or guided.

To be sure, the topographical configuration of a country, its size, and its geographical location on the earth's surface are not entirely irrelevant either when it comes to defending it against attack by aircraft and surface-to-surface missiles or—surprising as it may sound—launching missiles of its own.[19] For example, the 1999 NATO campaign against Serbia proved that a combination of forests, mountains, and decoys may conceal an entire army, even from the most modern airborne reconnaissance vehicles, at least as long as it keeps still and does not take an active part in operations. High mountains, especially if they are steep and separated by deep ravines, may also help. Owing to the trajectories on which they travel, ballistic missiles may find it harder to hit assets that are concealed in such a ravine. This is particularly true when the targets are relatively small, as in a counterforce strike. Seeking to base *its* missiles back in the 1960s and 1970s, China reportedly exploited this advantage. Tom Clancy, too, made use of it in order to spin his yarn, *A Debt of Honor,* making the Japanese place their force of intercontinental ballistic missiles in a ravine, and sending out a troupe of brave Americans to demolish the dam that blocked it.

Finally, a very large country may provide the defender with significantly more advance warning against attack. This is especially true if it is also an island, and especially if its main assets are located far from its borders and dispersed. Yet even that advantage should not be exaggerated. Take the U.S., which, thanks to its size and position between two oceans, enjoys it to an extent scarcely equaled by any other country on earth. All through the Cold War the U.S. spent tens of billions of dollars to build an enormous early warning system in the form of the North American Air Defense (NORAD). Relying on a chain of radar stations across Alaska and Canada, later supplemented by a global network of satellites, data-links, and the like, the best NORAD could do was to sound the alarm about half an hour before the Soviet missiles struck and turned their targets into radioactive rubble.[20] However, those thirty minutes would be reduced by more than two-thirds—to as few as seven or eight—if the Kremlin had chosen to open its offensive by attacking Washington D.C. with submarine-launched missiles traveling on "depressed" trajectories. Emergency plans for whisking away the president from the White House to Bolling Air Base and from there to his flying headquarters were based on the assumption that fifteen minutes' warning would be available. Which meant that, even if everything worked perfectly, not even the safety of the most important person on earth could be guaranteed; that everybody and everything else would have been incinerated does not require saying.

However important or unimportant such advantages may be, Israel does not enjoy any of them. It is not located at, nor does it have access to, a geographical line of latitude that may make it easier to launch missiles into space, set up satellite-tracking stations, or (perhaps, in the future) recover spacecraft returning from their missions. If anything, the opposite is the case. Just as Israel is always on the alert for a surprise attack, so its neighbors have been following its alleged ballistic missile program for years, and their radar stations are constantly sweeping the skies for them. To avoid false alarms, which may be dangerous to both sides and lead to accidental war, Israel has no choice but to launch its missile-carrying satellites westward over the Mediterranean against the direction of the earth's rotation. The price is that, for any given amount of thrust a booster generates, it will only be able to carry a somewhat smaller payload.

Nor does Israel have seas or oceans to separate it from its enemies, as many people no doubt wish it did. So small is the land mass it commands that any warning times it may obtain against air or missile attack must be very short; should it give up the West Bank and the Golan Heights, then at the very most those times will be decreased by a minute or so.[21] This is one reason why, already at present, part of the task of providing such warning is entrusted not to ground-based radar but to AWACS aircraft. It also explains why Israel's warplanes have long been housed in underground shelters; where, safe against surprise attack, they can be serviced and prepared for action. Though quite rugged, the mountains of Samaria and Judea are neither very extensive—they take up an area of less than a hundred by twenty miles—nor very high, nor very steep, nor covered with any vegetation to speak of. As a result, there is no way they can provide much cover for anything larger than small parties of terrorists.

Any Israeli attempt to use the Territories for deploying military assets has to start from the assumption that nothing can be hidden from the view of cameras in outer space. While it is true that no Arab or Moslem state has as yet followed Israel and launched a satellite, more and more of them are being put into orbit by private firms. Already

Arab intelligence services can purchase most of the images they need on the open market. They are hardly the only ones who do so;[22] even as the quality goes up, prices go down. Compared to the 8,000 or so square miles comprising Israel proper, the Occupied Territories only cover a total of 2,200 square miles. They are far too small and densely populated to permit much dispersion of military, let alone civilian, installations. Worse still, for several years past they have been rife with terrorist activity bordering on guerrilla warfare. Should the occupation continue, the situation is likely to deteriorate. Access to bases and depots may be impeded; turning them from assets into liabilities as most of the civilian settlements already are.

With or without weapons of mass destruction, as far as air and missile warfare are concerned whether or not Israel does or does not retain, does or does not rid itself of the Occupied Territories is largely irrelevant. To quote Weizman who, as an expert on air warfare, is as highly qualified as they come: "I am a pilot . . . where I operate, God's Covenant with Abraham [Genesis 15.13–21] is of no importance whatsoever."[23] A continued Israeli military presence on the watershed will not prevent drones from flying over from the east and spraying Tel Aviv with chemical or biological weapons. An Israeli presence in the Jordan Valley or the Golan Heights will not prevent a Syrian Scud missile, or an Iranian Shihab missile, from making its way to the same target. Nor will an Israeli presence in the Gaza Strip prevent similar missiles from being launched against it by Egypt, Libya, or anybody else who may wish to do so in the future. Insofar as these threats can be countered by a passive defense such as alarm systems, shelters, gas masks, antidotes, decontamination facilities, and the like, the Territories are totally irrelevant to them. Insofar as they can be countered by an active defense consisting of aircraft, antiballistic missiles, and, one day perhaps, directed-energy weapons, the Territories are also (almost) irrelevant to them.

The Israeli Air Force, which from the first days of the State has been responsible for protecting against hostile aircraft, requires such an extensive infrastructure that it can only be based in the coastal plain, the Negev, and the Valley of Esdraelon, all of which formed part of pre-1967 Israel. If only for reasons of security, the Israeli batteries of Arrow missiles which, in the spring of 2003, were being prepared for an eventual war against Iraq, were also based within the pre-1967 borders and not in the West Bank. So was the early-warning radar that served them. Whether, in the future, Israel will be able to afford more advanced antiballistic missile defenses—for example, such as rely on geostationary satellites to discover a missile being launched and use mid-course or boost-phase interception to destroy it—is, to say the least, doubtful. Even if the answer to this question turns out to be positive, whether or not it holds onto the West Bank will be irrelevant to the equation.

At present, Israel's defenses against aircraft and missiles are based on land. As in the case of the high-tech conventional forces described above, though, should the need arise they could also be based at least partly at sea. Whether because their enemies are situated across the water or for other reasons, the question of sea-based missile defenses preoccupies several other countries beside Israel. Among them are Japan, Taiwan, South Korea, and the U.S.; the latter is seeking a defense against sea-based cruise missiles.[24] Since some of these countries are already close to Israel, there may exist opportunities for cooperation, as in sharing the cost of Research and Development, common testing, and the like. While anything but cheap, an approach that would relocate the defense offshore has two very great advantages. First, seaborne platforms, being mobile over much larger areas, will be much harder to detect, track, and subject to a disarming first strike. Second, given the country's small size, a single platform might take care of an incoming attack launched not merely from the east, by Syria (and possibly Iran) but from the southwest, by Egypt and Libya, as well.

While the present version of the Arrow does not have the necessary range, prototypes of the necessary antiballistic missiles already exist abroad. In November 2002, one was successfully tested against a modified, single-stage Minuteman missile not too different from the ones that several Middle Eastern countries already possess or may acquire in the near future.[25] It has even been claimed that a single modified Aegis-type cruiser patrolling the eastern Mediterranean could take care of all these threats.[26] The interesting thing about this claim is that it originated in a former Israeli minister of internal security, Dr. Uzi Landau, a confirmed hawk who is determined to continue the occupation almost regardless of what the cost to his compatriots may be. If he can see, or thinks he can see, a way of defending Israel against missiles without holding on to the Territories, then anyone can.

The field where an eventual Israeli withdrawal from the Territories, and the West Bank in particular, *will* be relevant to the country's ability to withstand a long-range threat from aircraft and missiles is making sure that its forces can ride out an attack. Should the Territories be evacuated, then many of the bases where those aircraft in particular are located will become vulnerable to artillery and rocket (Katyusha) fire. In strictly military terms, such attacks will almost certainly represent mere pinpricks. On the other hand, so vital are the assets in question and so imperative the need to keep them in a state of instant readiness at all times that even pinpricks cannot be tolerated, but must be absolutely ruled out.

In view of everything said so far, the solution to the problem ought to be obvious. Whether or not Israel holds on to the Territories, it is imperative that some, perhaps most, of its strategic deterrent should be moved out to sea. Apparently the first high-ranking Israeli officer who seriously considered this possibility was General Ehud Barak when he was still deputy chief of staff in the late 1980s and early 1990s. At that time the scheme was frustrated by lack of money. American aid, remember, can only be spent buying American products in the U.S.; and the U.S. has long ceased building conventional-powered submarines such as Israel needs. However, one of the results of the 1991 Gulf War was to open some German purse strings. At present, Israel has three

Dolphin-class submarines which are among the most modern anywhere and which are said to be armed with nuclear-capable cruise missiles as their main weapons. Hence plans are afloat to have three additional ones built with American financial support, perhaps involving Taiwan as well, though whether the necessary arrangements can be worked out remains to be seen.[27]

Assuming the foreign reports are correct, how might Israel's missiles be targeted? On the declaratory level at any rate, U.S. nuclear doctrine since the 1960s has often focused on counterforce. By this was meant an attempt to knock out as many as possible of the Soviet Union's missiles and strategic bombers before they could be launched; which was why, as against 1,000 Minuteman missiles with their multiple warheads, the force only included fifty-four Titan city busters. Even in the American case, whether such a doctrine was ever really practical is doubtful; had just a single one of the warheads carried by the Minuteman missiles gone astray, then the outcome would have been Armageddon. Be this as it may, as far as Israel's needs go such a use would represent gross waste. Whereas the number of American and Soviet Intercontinental Ballistic Missiles (ICBMs) was approximately equal, Arab missiles, being quite cheap, outnumber Israel's several times over. To the extent that they carry chemical warheads rather than nuclear ones, those warheads are also much cheaper; an attempt to use Israel's own missiles against them will therefore be extremely wasteful. Third, whereas most Soviet ICBMs were housed in silos and could be knocked out, at least in principle, many Arab missiles are mobile and much easier to conceal. All these considerations point to the adoption of a doctrine centering on counter-value.

As somebody said long ago, nuclear weapons, like ice cream, may be had in any color and taste. They may be tailored to deliver either blast or radiation, either nonpersistent or persistent radiation; or else, if that were the objective, an electromagnetic pulse (EMP) strong enough to knock out every electronic device for miles around.[28] Just one warhead, delivered at the right spot well ahead of an enemy force, could create either a physical obstacle or a radioactive one that only the most foolhardy would dare approach and that could cause enemy troops who are forced to approach it to mutiny. For example, it would be possible to block some pass for days—if all that were needed to clear the fallen rock was heavy earth-moving equipment—or else for weeks, months, or even years; in strategic lingo, doing so is known as "area denial."

To be sure, this is not a simple option. Using nuclear weapons never is, both in itself (the possibility of fallout and radiation must be taken into account) and because of the international complications that will inevitably follow; to say nothing of the likelihood that he who lives by the sword will, sooner or later, be killed by it. Therefore, presumably it will be reserved for the most desperate circumstances. Not just a limited surprise attack, like the one that took place in October 1973 and did not penetrate Israel's own borders, but a massive, successful offensive clearly aimed at Jerusalem, Haifa, and Tel Aviv. Not one whose outcome might be a local defeat, but one that might lead to politicide and, perhaps, genocide as well. As of the time of writing the balance of forces as well as the fact that Israel is at peace with both Egypt and Jordan makes such an offensive appear more unlikely than it has been at any time since the first Zionists started returning to the Land of Israel. Should it take place one day, then the beautiful thing about this option is that the areas around the passes are home to little but a few camels. Both in the Sinai and in the east-Jordanian hills there will be hardly any civilian casualties and no collateral damage to speak of. Except perhaps in Russian Siberia, which geographically speaking is equally open to a (Chinese) invasion and equally empty of people, one can think of few other places on earth where tactical nuclear weapons, if they exist, could be used to such good effect at such low cost.

Finally, will the possession of nuclear weapons enable Israel to deter large-scale military attack by neighboring countries? In the past, much ink has been spilt to answer that question.[29] Many fine distinctions were drawn between sophisticated nuclear arsenals and crude ones, such as might be activated by mistake and such as were protected by American-type PALs (Passive Action Links) which supposedly provided a guarantee against such a possibility. Then there were symmetric and asymmetric threats, bipolar and multipolar balances of power, large and small states. Most important of all, there were "rational" states and "crazy" ones; that the Arab World supposedly had more than its share of the latter goes without saying.[30] Incidentally, one of those who, during the late 1950s and early 1960s, accused Arab rulers of being driven by irrational motives that might, in case they themselves developed nuclear weapons, cause them to do strange things was Yigal Allon. Paradoxically he also claimed that an Israeli nuclear option might lead to a balance of terror in the Middle East and thus to the existing borders, which he regarded as "defective," being frozen. This, in his view, would obviate Israel's conventional superiority; preventing the State from expanding if and when the opportunity presented itself.[31]

In the Middle East and elsewhere the nuclear debate has a Talmudistic quality about it, and hence I shall not bother the readers with these distinctions, many of which are either tinted with racism or simply wrong. In the Middle East and elsewhere, the plain fact is that deterrence is working and has done so for a considerable time in the past. Between 1948 and 1982, a period of thirty-four years, the Israeli Army fought five—six, if the "War of Attrition" is included—major wars, i.e. one every seven years, on the average. As a result, until the early 1980s that army was perhaps the most experienced anywhere. Generations of warriors grew up, were conscripted, fought, bled, and, like flowers in a pot, faded away and were succeeded by others. From the late 1960s on, it also served as a laboratory where some of the world's most advanced weapons and tactics were tried for the first time. The first time this happened was during "the first electronic war" of 1969–1970, when American avionics were imported and used against Egyptian antiaircraft missiles, with mixed results. It happened again in 1973, and, much more spectacularly, in 1982. In the last-named campaign Israel revealed, and some at the time thought threw away, a whole series of technological breakthroughs. They ranged from reactive armor (the first to see service anywhere) to UAVs; and from electronic countermeasures to air-to-surface missiles.[32]

Since then, things have changed. Apart from the First Gulf War, to be discussed in a moment, so successful has deterrence been that I challenge anybody to name the last time when an Israeli pilot shot down an Arab combat aircraft, or when the Israeli Air Force in turn lost an aircraft in action.[33] It is true that small-scale, anti-terrorist operations, some of them overt and others covert, are going on practically without interruption. Sometimes they yield very good results, as happened in the winter of 2002 when the IDF intercepted a ship that carried arms for the PLO. On the other hand, in the entire 500,000-strong force there is now hardly an officer left who has commanded as much as a battalion fighting a regular Arab army; this even applies to the Chief of Staff. Particularly on the Southern Front, which used to be the most important one and where generals spent their time preparing to fight or actually fighting the Egyptians, their successors now act more as policemen than as anything else. Except perhaps in the field of counterguerrilla and counterterrorism, where its performance has been no better than average, nobody anymore looks to Israel as a source of military doctrine, or sees it as a battle laboratory, or seeks to learn from the campaigns it fought. Nor can Israel's military industries, trying to export their wares, honestly claim that many of them have been "battle tested." Faute de mieux, often they are forced to rely on maneuvers and simulations instead.

Mirror-wise, what applies to Israel applies equally well to many of its opponents. Some of them may be quite belligerent, even bloodthirsty. This does not change the fact that, over the last two decades, they too have had scant opportunity to flex their military muscle, waging war on the hated Zionist Entity. With very few exceptions, the most they have done is to support terrorists. Though some of the resulting acts of terrorism have been somewhat spectacular, in the end even that support has been limited. No Arab ruler is known to have provided terrorists either with effective long-range weapons—those in the hands of Hizbollah have no more than a nuisance value—or with weapons of mass destruction. Doing so would be tantamount to putting their own fate and that of their countries in the hands of people over whom they have no control and who, in some cases, are known for their willingness to take risks; hence they are unlikely to do so in the future either. Some Arab commentators go much further still. They accuse their leaders of having given up the struggle and surrendered their ideals rather than confront Israel, as was their sacred duty.[34]

Like their opposite numbers elsewhere, Arab leaders are probably not familiar with every detail of deterrence theory which some of them have discussed in the crudest of terms. Still, when it comes to nuclear weapons crude does not necessarily mean wrong; terms such as "extended immediate deterrence" may be meaningful, if at all, only to the political scientists who invented them. However that may be, there is no doubt that the leaders in question are as aware of what nuclear weapons may do, and as fearful of the consequences that using them may bring, as anybody else.[35] At least since 1973, much of what they have and have not done can only be understood against this background. The same is true of Iran. The only modern Iranian figure capable of inspiring the people to extraordinary sacrifices, Ayatollah Ruhollah Khomeini, left the stage years ago. Perhaps because they have become used to power and have more to lose, his successors are both less fanatical and less irrational than they are sometimes said to be. Their principal concern is survival, which in view of repeated and massive domestic unrest represents no easy task, the more so because some of the unrest appears to be stimulated from outside. All in all they show few signs of being crazier than anybody else. What motivates them is the national interest as they understand it, not some extraordinary desire to reach Heaven ahead of the appointed time.[36]

It is true that the Arab states that matter are much larger than Israel and that it will take more to inflict "unacceptable damage" on them. However, it is also true that, as far back as 1986, foreign sources estimated Israel's nuclear arsenal at no fewer than 200 weapons. More recent estimates, also published by foreign sources, range from 100 to as many as 400.[37] They are said to fall into four (five, if the earliest prototype is included) distinct types ranging from 0.2 to 200 kilotons;[38] the latter figure means a weapon fifteen times more powerful than the one that annihilated Hiroshima and ten times more than the one that obliterated Nagasaki. Even if one accepts the lowest number of bombs, Israel would still be capable of wiping out not just any single Arab state but a coalition made up of several states. What is more, the very asymmetry that makes it so hard for Israel to translate its conventional military power into a political victory also means that, for the Arab states, the conflict with Israel has an instrumental character. It is not their existence that is at stake but their political objectives only. Other things being equal, this fact should make deterrence much easier to exercise.

To make matters worse for them, most of Israel's neighbors are centralized both demographically and politically. On the one hand, being underdeveloped, a larger percentage of their populations live in the countryside, scratching the earth and herding their goats as their ancestors have always done; few places on earth are as poor and as underdeveloped as Egyptian villages. On the other, they tend to contain one or two cities—Cairo and Alexandria, Damascus and Homs, Tehran and Khom, Jedda and Riad—which are far larger and symbolically more important than the rest. The destruction of these cities would be tantamount to the annihilation of their societies, reducing them to an Afghanistan-like rabble of warring tribes, clans, and families—not just politicide but culticide as well. The experience of other countries since 1945 also shows that, to prevent the outbreak of war, the damage on both sides does not have to be symmetrical. As the French strategist

Andre Beaufre used to say, to deter somebody from trying to kill you it is enough if you are able to tear off his arm.

Another factor that distinguishes Arab rulers from many others is their concern with their own survival and that of their relatives. Most of them owe their position to force rather than democratic elections. For most of them continued, not to say continuous, use of force is a prerequisite for staying in power, and in case they lose it they cannot expect to retire to private life and die in their beds. To put it in a different way, for them the personal and the political are linked in ways that they are not in other, more developed, societies; a separation between the two is both impossible and inconceivable. That these attitudes play a large part in governing their policies and shaping their regimes is beyond doubt. In our context it is possible, as some commentators have suggested,[39] that they may also be carried over into the field of nuclear deterrence. If this is true, then Arab leaders, their families (who, as in Syria, Iraq, and perhaps Egypt, themselves form part of the power structure) and the elites that support them and are the principal beneficiaries of their rule may be easier to deter than their opposite numbers in other countries. Provided, of course, their capitals and the bunkers where they may hide are targeted by the appropriate weapons; and provided, of course, measures are taken to make it clear to them what their fate might be.

To illustrate these generalities with the aid of a concrete example, take the captured unlamented Saddam Hussein. Like so many Arab leaders, Saddam came to power by means of a coup and consolidated it by means of an intricate network of supporters, many of whom were relatives or came from the same town as he himself did. Of all the Arab leaders, he was the one who placed the greatest reliance on military force to achieve his goals. He spent tens of billions building up his army, put it on parade for the benefit of Iraqis and foreigners alike, and directed several major counterinsurgency campaigns against his own people. He invaded not one but two of his neighbors, made threats against several others, and ended up fighting the Mother of all Battles against a global coalition. Though his own rise to the top led through the Secret Service rather than the army, personally he was as militaristic as they come. Facing the cameras, much of the time he dressed in uniform and made his closest collaborators do the same, causing his Revolutionary Council to look less like the government of a modern state than like a group of gnomes conspiring together. Repeatedly he brandished weapons in public, cocked them, and fired them into the air. Even in the Arab world, where glorifying war is considered more acceptable than in the West and where TV images of battlefields are often accompanied by stirring music, this is no longer something heads of state do every day.

By nature Saddam was a gambler. He was always at his best when the odds were stacked against him, playing his cards with ruthlessness and skill. One good example was the spring of 1983, when it looked as if Basra might fall to the Iranians; another, eight years later in the aftermath of the First Gulf War, when he succeeded in maintaining his rule and putting down two uprisings at once.[40] There were also moments when, feeling strong, he was carried away and engaged in blustering. Repeatedly he promised to lead crusades against Israel, reminding his listeners of what King Nebuchadnezzar had done to the ancient kingdom of Judea and also of the fact that Saladin was a native of Tikrit, as he himself was. Once, in the spring of 1990, he threatened "to burn down half of Israel." What has been less widely reported, though, was that he promptly qualified his declaration, saying that it only applied "in case Israel attacks a certain [Iraqi] industrial metalwork."[41] Presumably what he had in mind were his nuclear installations; was it an accident that, in an oblique reference to its own nuclear program many years earlier, Israel itself had used the very same words?[42] On other occasions, too, Saddam always took care to retract his more extreme statements on nuclear weapons almost immediately after they were made.[43] Either he did so because his advisers warned him that he was getting himself into deep water, or because making threats and then withdrawing them was part of some game he liked to play.

Be this as it may, when the crunch came Saddam turned out to be no more irresponsible or crazy than anybody else. To the contrary, he was very careful not to overstep the line, making sure that the forty-three missiles he launched at Israel during the 1991 War should carry conventional warheads only. Partly for this reason, partly because many Israelis had taken the initiative and evacuated the cities in which they lived, and partly by sheer chance the damage they did was very limited. In all, only three people were killed; another seven died of heart attacks or as a result of putting on their gas masks in the wrong way. Two missiles were aimed in the direction of Dimona, more or less, but a post-mortem examination of their remains showed that they had been "armed" with warheads made of concrete and building steel. Some years later the commander of Iraq's missile force, General Hazam a-Razek al Ayubi, wrote a book in which he justified this by quoting a myth according to which some birds assisted Allah's champions, bombarding the infidel with stones.[44] More likely it was meant to ensure that, in case the reactor were hit, no major damage would be done. Radiation might, indeed, reach as far as Iraq itself, affecting that country in the way the Chernobyl disaster affected northwestern Europe. Furthermore, an effective attack on the reactor might have caused Israel to resort to its nuclear option—always assuming it does in fact have them—in return, which could easily have spelled the end of Iraq as well as Saddam personally.

Again, this is hardly the place to discuss the finer points of a would-be Israeli nuclear doctrine. Such a discussion would have to include such questions as open, declared deterrence versus the current "bomb in the basement" policy. It would also include deterrence versus punishment on the one hand and coercion on the other; first use versus second use; launch upon impact versus launch upon warning; counterforce versus countervalue; the possibility, or lack of it, of "broken back" warfare; and many similar questions.[45] Whether Israel's top-level civilian leaders are better informed about these problems than their opposite numbers elsewhere is unknown. The fact that so many of them have spent much of their careers in the military makes one hope that they have devoted at least some thought to them, though this is far from certain. Whatever the discussions they may hold among themselves behind closed doors, it must be admitted that, in the past, they have been very careful not to issue any statements on the matter, and prudence demands that they refrain from doing so in the future, too. In part, this is because too much irresponsible talk might push some Arabs, the Egyptians in particular, to think of going nuclear, a development that would not be welcomed in Israel. In part it is because of the need to avoid trouble with the U.S., which, for its own reasons, has long been doing whatever it could to prevent nuclear weapons from spreading to countries in the Middle East and elsewhere.

In any case, given that no nuclear weapon has been dropped in anger since 1945, much of this is as academic as Medieval debates about the number of angels who could dance on the head of a pin. The point I wish to make is simply that, should Israel one day decide to evacuate the Territories and return to its previous borders, then the Middle East unconventional balance of terror will not be affected to any appreciable extent. Far from a withdrawal weakening deterrence, the latter may be strengthened. This is because any attack will now have to be directed against Israel's own territory rather than a buffer zone. Hence it will be much more likely to evoke a response on Israel's part; any Arab leader who launches such a strike will have to be either mad or hellbent on destroying his own capital, complete with most of its inhabitants. To be sure, a withdrawal *will* reinforce the need to redeploy as much as possible of Israel's strategic forces at sea, complete with all the changes in the balance between the three services that such a shift will bring, and complete also with the very considerable bill. Basically, though, that need is the result of completely different factors. For all these reasons that redeployment will have to be carried out in any case, regardless of whether or not the Territories remain under Israeli control.

eaving these almost purely military considerations for political, economic, social, and technological ones, a withdrawal to a wall running along the pre-1967 border, more or less, combined with a defense of the kind here proposed, will also offer other advantages. Perhaps the most important one is the prospect of finally overcoming some of Israel's own inner political problems. At present Israelis, including those who wear uniform and carry high rank,[1] are divided as they have been for more than three decades past. On the one hand are the peaceniks. Some of them are true bleeding hearts, and some of them specialize in peddling sympathy instead of strategy. They believe that an agreement with the Arabs—including, above all, the Palestinians—is possible in principle and are willing to make far-reaching "concessions" to that end. They tend to belittle the importance of Palestinian terrorism, claiming it is the work of a handful of "peace-hating" extremists, presenting it as if it were of no consequence, and even seeking excuses for it. No wonder they never obtained a mass following, particularly among the lower classes and particularly among less-educated people. Even in 1994, in the afterglow of the Oslo Agreements, over half of Israelis polled thought the Arabs' ultimate goal was to destroy Israel.[2] During the last weeks before his death Rabin himself barely commanded a majority in Parliament; indeed, Benjamin Netanyahu, who was highly critical of the Agreements, was running ahead of him in the polls. Is it any wonder that, since the outbreak of the Second Uprising, their numbers have been declining and the Labor Party that claims to represent them has dwindled?

On the other side stand the hard-liners represented by Likud and some other parties even further to the right. Following an ideology that long antedates the State, they insist that all Arabs, and the Palestinians in particular, are determined to destroy Israel and throw the Jews into the sea as the PLO's first chairman, Ahmed Shukeiry, once put it. If not immediately and in a single fell swoop, then in the long run and phase by phase, using salami tactics; and if not by open warfare then by the time-tested method of talk-talk, fight-fight. From this it follows that any concessions Israel makes in return for Arab promises can only weaken its position when, as inevitably happens sooner or later, those promises are broken and the struggle is resumed; survival depends on hanging on, come what may. Some go much further still. They link the Arabs' determination to do away with Israel to alleged faults in their religious beliefs, psychological makeup, social system, education system, treatment of women, and what not, and swear one can never conclude peace with such bad, bad people.[3] Thus the Left accuses the Right of having no heart; the Right the Left, of having no brain.

The plan here outlined seeks to solve the impasse and permit political action by not postulating Palestinian goodwill—supposing there is any left after years of bloody repression—for its realization and by refusing to make *any* concessions as a way to gaining it. Like most Israelis this author hopes that the Palestinians and other Arabs will one day change their fundamental attitudes toward Israel which, at present, range all the way from grudging acceptance and willingness to maintain a "cold" peace to rejection in principle. Either they do so, or they don't. Either the Palestinians succeed in overcoming their internal divisions, setting up a government, negotiating an agreement, and enforcing compliance with it, or they don't. Either the lamb lies down with the lion, or it does not. Until all this takes place, to quote a famous saying by Ben Gurion, what matters is not what the Gentiles may say but what the Jews will do.[4]

To put the idea as bluntly as I can, the entire notion of "concessions" is false and should be thrown overboard as fast as possible. Partly to be on the safe side, partly to please Israel's hawks, the working assumption should be that the hawks are right. If not in practice then certainly in theory, and if not in the short term then as certainly in the long one; as Ben Gurion in his more somber moments used to say, no people gives up its land in favor of another. Consequently, an agreement with the Palestinians is impossible. Even if it can be reached, it can only be trusted within certain limits and for the time being. Precisely *because* they are right and an agreement can only be trusted within certain limits, any move Israel makes should be aimed at maximizing its own power. It should not try to please the moderate Palestinians, or the hard-line Palestinians, or any other Arabs, from Morocco to the Persian Gulf. It is for that reason, and for that reason alone, that Israel should seek to rid itself of as much Palestinian ballast as possible. Once this is done the remaining threat can be dealt with by military rather than police methods; the faster the shift is made, the better.

As Israel does so, the guiding principle should be that immediate perils—in other words, terrorism and its consequences—are more important than future ones, such as the possible reconstruction of powerful Arab armies at some remote date; also it should not be forgotten that human beings are more important than geography. Ours, after all, is a democratic age, when all nations are supposed to be equal and every inch of the land they live on is ipso facto rendered sacred and inviolable. "Annexation" has become the dirtiest of all dirty words, only exceeded by "subjugation"; what used to be known as the "right of conquest" has turned into an oxymoron. From 1945 on, the whole of military experience proves that few if any "strategic" areas are worth the expense of ruling the population that lives on them against that population's will. In other words that occupation, instead of being a source of strength for a state, will only cause it to bleed.

It is of course possible that some of the Palestinian organizations, mistaking Israel's power in carrying out the withdrawal for weakness, may think it invites more terrorism and try to continue their attacks regardless of the wall. If so then that power, now liberated from the responsibility of looking after the occupied population, can be demonstrated once again at the right moment and in the right way. Just what such a demonstration might mean I leave to the reader's imagination. For those who are interested in the question, Niccolo Machiavelli, in *The Prince,* has some useful advice to offer;[5] compared to the residents of Lebanon, who were always able to go one mile further north, the Palestinians in the Gaza Strip and the West Bank will have nowhere to escape. The outcome will be to cut the Gordian knot as each of the two main Israeli camps obtains what, in its view, is the most important objective of all. Namely peace, or at any rate quiet, on the one hand, and security against further terrorist attacks on the other.

Next comes the question of how to deal with the settlements in the Occupied Territories. Back in the spring of 1982, when Begin and Sharon returned the Sinai, and especially the town of Yamit, to Egypt, there were ugly scenes as settlers fought the soldiers who had come to evacuate them from their homes. Some used makeshift weapons, such as planks, causing injuries, although none that were terribly severe. Others kept returning and had to be evacuated several times over; the fact that all this took place in full view of the TV cameras did not make things easier. Today, too, there is no shortage of right-wing rabbis who would be happy to proclaim resistance to evacuation, including, perhaps, active resistance, a religious duty.[6] Some fear that, should there be a repetition, the outcome could be civil war as settlers defend their homes and orthodox IDF soldiers refuse to carry out their orders.[7] This possibility is magnified by the media, which always focus on the violent minority while ignoring the silent majority.

Once again, the plan here outlined presents a way out. Instead of starting its move by evacuating the settlers one by one—which, given their numbers, is impractical anyhow—Israel should show everybody where the wind is blowing by completing the wall as fast as possible. Next, the Government should announce that it intends to withdraw from those parts of the Territories that are not included in the wall by such and such a date. To show it means business, it should also start making practical preparations towards that goal; dismantling bases, removing equipment, and the like. As the settlers watch the army units on whom their lives depend pull out, they will be promised state help in finding new places to live. To be sure, keeping the promise will not be cheap; over more than thirty years, so many billions have been wasted settling the Territories that finding more money to evacuate them is surely going to be anything but easy. Nevertheless, the country that, between 1991 and 1999, absorbed about a million new immigrants from Russia and elsewhere should not find it too difficult to find room for 200,000 of its own people as well. Both in the south and in the north there are areas that cry out for additional Jewish citizens, and which, unless they are populated with Jews, may end up lost to the State. A wall will also make it possible to remove such settlers as will have to be evacuated against their will to its other side, rather than play cat-and-mouse games with them as the IDF is doing at present.

To be sure, the strength of the human feelings that evacuation will evoke should not be underestimated. Still, chances are that the overwhelming majority will decide to leave of their own accord. Failure to do so will bring them face-to-face with an Arab population that far outnumbers them and hates them as only a colonial people can hate its masters; even now, some are complaining about what a wall will do to their security. These settlers are where they are not for religious or ideological reasons but because of the opportunity, deliberately created by the Begin Government and maintained since then, to acquire cheap housing at the Palestinians' expense. The difference in cost is about 35 percent; on top of this the settlers enjoy very considerable tax breaks, "location-specific" loans that do not have to be repaid after so and so many years, and the like. On a per capita basis, government spending in the Territories exceeds the sums invested inside the so-called "Green Line" by more than two to one. Particularly in the larger settlements, the outcome is often a high quality of life with very good roads (those that are not targeted by snipers), beautiful schools, parks, country clubs, and the like. All this has turned many of the settlements into magnets for people without means. Many are lower middle class—as one would expect, there are very few upper-class people living in the Territories—out for the additional room and a nice patch of a garden. Others are young, usually religious, bachelors just out of the army who tend to occupy many of the "footholds." Others still are recent immigrants on the lookout for a place where the mortgages the government gives them may buy the most property. There are even some single mothers with their broods; while many are understandably attached to their homes, it is equally true that many, perhaps most, are no more hawkish than the average Israeli is.

Almost one-third of the settlers, constantly harassed and shot at, are prepared to get out even now,[8] and are only held back by the impossibility of selling their homes and the cost of purchasing new ones. Others take a more cynical view, seeing the places where they live as little more than vacation houses with a built-in option for compensation if and when the time comes. Like the one-time residents of Yamit, they delay their departure for as long as possible in the hope of obtaining it; had the government *wanted* to give them an incentive to demonstrate their opposition to any evacuation, then present policies would have been ideally designed to accomplish that purpose.

Yet for all the inflammatory talk there is another side to the matter. About one-quarter of the settlers consist of orthodox families whose fertility is exceptionally high and who, if only for that reason, are always looking for new places where they can lead their peculiar way of life without being disturbed by their neighbors. They alone are responsible for such an increase in the Jewish population in the West Bank and the Gaza Strip as still takes place; as far as migration is concerned, since 2000 more Jews have been moving out of the Territories then there were new ones coming into them.[9] The tenuous nature of the settlers' presence was made clear by the fact that, no sooner was the sound of distant peace bells heard in the spring of 2003, then purchases of new homes dropped by 95 percent compared to a year earlier.[10] A few months later things got so bad that Sharon started offering homes in the Jordan Valley for free.[11]

Recent polls show that fewer than 10 percent (i.e. about 20,000), of the settlers expect to actively resist evacuation if and when it comes. The figure appears large but is greatly exaggerated. This is because the only people surveyed are adults, and in some settlements children under eighteen comprise almost two-thirds of the population. At the other end of the spectrum as many as 90 percent say they won't resist. Seventy-five percent think that peace is a necessity. Eighty percent are prepared to accept compensation and leave, 66 percent think illegal footholds should be evacuated, and 44 percent believe that the Palestinians deserve a State of their own. To put the icing on the cake, 75 percent say that the settler's self-appointed "leadership," which tends towards extremism, does not represent them.[12]

In any case, polls can do no more than reflect the way people expect to act or what they say about the way they expect to act. Perhaps the best indicator of the settlers' real intentions is the fact that, already now, many of them bury their dead—both those who were killed by terrorists and those who died of other causes—inside "old" Israel, as the phrase goes. This even applies to some of the religious fanatics who have occupied living quarters in the middle of the ancient city of Hebron. They proclaim the need to take up where the patriarch Abraham left off almost four millennia ago; yet deep in their hearts even they know very well how the adventure is going to end. Perhaps it is fortunate that, by Rabbinical Law, disturbing a grave is prohibited and that, in Hebrew, the expression "behind the fence" carries ominous overtones; to realize that, one only has to listen to some of the settlers denouncing the fence on the radio.

With or without a formal peace, the immediate effect of a withdrawal will be to release vast numbers of Israelis from the need to chase terrorists around. To illustrate what this means, in mid-2003 the West Bank alone required no less than six so-called "regional" brigades (meaning stationary ones with much of their rear-echelon services stripped away) controlled by a divisional headquarters.[13] The Gaza Strip, which is only about 140 square miles in size and whose population is smaller than that of the West Bank by one half, is nevertheless controlled by another divisional headquarters and policed by three brigades. Compare this to the June 1967 War when it took just eleven brigades only four days to smash the entire Egyptian Army. Once upon a time an Israeli armored company defeated an Arab battalion before going on to defeat the next one; nowadays a similar force is needed simply to make sure Mr. Arafat does not leave his Ramallah compound. In May 2003, to ferret out a handful of terrorists in the northern Gaza township of Beth Hannoun, two armored battalions with about sixty tanks and several times that number of other vehicles went into action for two days. To these vast forces must be added the daily use of UAVs, observation aircraft, attack helicopters, and, from time to time, attack aircraft and missile boats as well. All are among the most sophisticated anywhere. No wonder that, as a percentage of GDP, defense spending is about as high now as it was before 1967, when Israel still lived within "insecure" borders.

In and outside the Territories, on any given day for every place that comes under attack there are perhaps a thousand that must be fortified to some degree and watched. For every terrorist who goes on a mission lasting, say, a few hours and ending either in success (as he or she makes his getaway or blows himself or herself up) or failure (as he or she is killed or captured), there may be as many as a hundred guards. Compare this to the time when, as mentioned above, one Israeli soldier was considered to be equivalent to three and a half Palestinians in battle— and when, of all the Arab troops, Palestinians were considered the worst. If these figures are even nearly correct, then switching from regular warfare to counterterrorism has caused the effectiveness of the

Israeli armed forces to decrease by well over 90 percent; seldom have so many, fighting so few, achieved so little at such cost. Nor, in view of what happened and is happening to other armies in similar situations, is this decline at all surprising.

While the IDF is trying to empty the ocean by using a teaspoon—the metaphor comes from a former chief of the Security Service, General (ret.) Amiel Ayalon—its lack of success is reflected in the fact that the number of private security firms has mushroomed to around three hundred. While the economy is in the grip of the worst recession in the country's history—in the twelve months from June 2002 alone the average monthly wage has declined by 8 percent,[14] and this was before salary cuts in the public service went into effect—for them business is booming. One firm, Hashmira Inc., has grown into the single largest employer in Israel. It has 15,000 employees, which is more than the National Electricity Company, Israel Aircraft Industries, or Israel Telecommunications (Bezek). The top sixteen private security companies alone employ 50,000 people. Their combined turnover is half a billion dollars a year, which means that their productivity per employee is only one tenth of that of a properly run commercial or industrial firm. One does not know whether to laugh or to cry; the less efficient a company and the less it actually produces, the better apparently for the balance sheet. Yet even these numbers, preposterous as they are, do not include the groups of vigilantes who, riding light combat vehicles and heavily armed, rampage through the Territories, beating up people, destroying property, and creating havoc. Also excluded are members of the various security services, the Frontier Guard (itself the size of a small division, and growing all the time), the ordinary police, and any number of specialized units that watch everything from buses or electricity pylons to railway tracks. Most of whom are kept so busy doing nothing that, in the words of a former minister for internal security, they barely manage to stay on their feet.

At any one time the vast majority of these people are where they are not because intelligence has sounded the alarm or pinpointed a threat but simply because, in the absence of a specific warning, everybody wants to have his back covered in case something does happen. Ill selected—a few were found to be former inmates of lunatic asylums—ill trained—training costs money—ill equipped—some of them cannot be trusted with guns—and ill paid, they hang around twenty-four hours a day, seven days a week. Many are elderly because the elderly come cheap. For the same reason, many are new immigrants who, since they cannot speak the language properly, would be unable to identify a terrorist if he walked up to them and told them who he was. All of them spend their time waiting, if that is the word, for an incident that, thank goodness, still takes place less frequently than do traffic accidents; as a result, most of the time they are bored half to death. This in turn means that they look for any diversion to make their task more interesting and are easily distracted from performing it. Normally all that is needed is a few loud words and/or a nice pair of legs; nor does the fact that Israelis are perhaps the least disciplined people on earth help.

If the guards do their work in a perfunctory manner it is worse than useless, creating a false sense of security where there is none. Not to mention the possibility, which has actually been realized on several occasions, that they may kill the wrong person by mistake, doing more psychological damage in an hour than a hundred propagandists can repair in a year. If they do the job thoroughly, passersby are harassed at every step. This causes the whole of social life to slow down, making people reluctant to leave their homes and helping depress many kinds of economic activity, from movie houses to restaurants; over the last three years the number of the latter has fallen by half.

From time to time the guards' well-intended efforts, perhaps triggered by a simple telephone call, result in monumental traffic jams; when it comes to creating confusion a fake threat may be just as effective as, though far cheaper than, a genuine one. On such occasions the police are alerted and the roadblocks go up. Hundreds, perhaps thousands of drivers are asked for their papers, the numbers on car-license plates are registered, and so on. For the day-to-day effects, I invite readers to watch the shopping center near where I myself live; here, too, lack of discipline plays a role, making the confusion even greater than it need be. Last but not least, compared to the Palestinians Israel's labor force is much better educated and more expensive. Low as it is, a guard's hourly pay of about six dollars will feed a resident of the Territories for a whole day; a less efficient way of using their time and energy could hardly be imagined.

Numbers apart, a withdrawal would mean that Israel's Defense Force—based as it is on the country's civilian population—will no longer have to spend themselves in a futile attempt to "fight" an opponent so much weaker than itself that he is all but invisible. As the experience of the French in Algeria, the Soviets in Afghanistan, the Indonesians in East Timor, and countless others shows, such a policy corrodes the forces that carry it out. In the words of an ancient Chinese sage, Lao-Tzu: "a sword, plunged into salt water, *will* rust." It weakens their fighting spirit, depresses their prestige to the point where attracting high-quality manpower becomes all but impossible, and undermines discipline. In Israel today nobody knows or wants to know how many soldiers have either refused to serve in the Territories or used various excuses in order not to do reserve duty; clearly the number is in the tens of thousands.

Another thing that counterinsurgency does is to open the door for vandals, thieves, extortionists, sadists, and perverts of every kind to realize their fantasies at the expense of the hapless population. From October 2000 to June 2003 alone, 360 Israeli soldiers were put under investigation, an average of two per week. Among them were 153 cases of suspected homicide and 34 of theft. In one case a female soldier allegedly put a gun to a Palestinian woman's head, forcing her to drink a poisonous liquid;[15] in July 2003 a complete Border Guard company was dismantled as many of its troops were accused of committing war crimes. Yet these figures almost certainly represent just one-tenth of the tip of the proverbial iceberg. As even the army's Judge Advocate General admits,[16] for every complaint that is registered there are a thousand that are not; standard legal methods are simply overwhelmed by the size of the problem at hand. Conversely, for every abuse that takes place in reality a thousand are invented out of thin air. The rumors about them spread, enraging the population, reinforcing its determination to resist, and helping depress the counterinsurgents' image both in their own eyes and in those of others. Worst of all, the more atrocities the troops commit, the more likely they are to lie in order to cover their own tracks, and those of their comrades, against any television camera that may happen to be around. The outcome is a never-never land where situation reports and the orders that are based on them are systematically falsified and no longer reflect reality. Compare the situation of the U.S. Army during the last years of the Vietnam War; when tens of thousands went AWOL and an estimated one-third of the troops were on hard drugs.[17]

As the commissions of investigation that are set up after each successful terrorist incident prove, Israel, too, is not immune to this danger. As in other countries caught in similar situations, soldiers have sought to salve their consciences by accusing their superiors of forcing them to commit war crimes.[18] As in other countries, attempts to put soldiers on trial gave rise to an entire industry; not for nothing is the acronym LIC (Low Intensity Conflict) sometimes said to stand for Lawyer Infested Conflict. For every news item that describes the army favorably, there are perhaps ten negative ones that focus on neglect, putative war crimes, or both. The public appetite seems insatiable and some journalists refuse to print or air anything else; throughout the Uprising, hardly a day passed without this or that "misdeed" being made the subject of an exposé. As a former chief of staff, General Amnon Shachak, put it some years ago, the IDF has become "the national punching bag";[19] since then, the only thing that has changed is that they have become used to it.

Carrying these attitudes to an extreme, some bereaved parents have openly accused commanders of murdering their sons, and others demand that that "fact" be recorded on the dead mens' graves. The day when every other Israeli child used to dress up as a soldier at Purim, the equivalent of Halloween, is long gone. So is the time when walls throughout the country were covered with graffiti calling on people to "Doff their hats to IDF." When I tell my students that such used to be the case they refuse to believe their ears; whether this is because or in spite of the fact that most of them have served in it is not clear.

By contrast, an end to the occupation would allow the army's prestige, and its mental balance, to recover—as, incidentally, also happened to some extent after it evacuated most of Lebanon in 1985. The process whereby it is gradually slipping away from civilian control may be halted and, hopefully, reversed. Its personnel will be able to take a deep breath. The troops can start retraining for the kind of serious warfare that, whether because they have no time or because they have become accustomed to chasing terrorists, they have all but forgotten how to wage. For example, daily experience in the Gaza Strip and elsewhere has turned Israeli tankers into world champions in handling their vehicles, technically speaking. They know how to drive them through narrow, winding streets and alleys, avoid most landmines, aim their guns to pick out individual targets even at night, and create the kind of mayhem that supposedly has a deterrent effect on the inhabitants. Its infantrymen know just how to break into a house, conduct a search, and handcuff suspects; its helicopter crews can pick up an individual car in the traffic, aim a missile at it, and demolish it together with its passengers. On the other hand, years have passed since they, or their commanders, saw training in large formations or seriously tested their rear-echelon services.[20] All this is reflected in military parlance that speaks of "heavy fighting" each time a few grenades are lobbed at a bunker or an antitank rocket is fired at it; as in any sport, the absence of real opposition causes the players to adapt their game to what is available. Fortunately for Israel, the day when its troops will be called upon to confront a real enemy armed with heavy machine guns, tanks, and cannon appears remote. Should it come nevertheless, then how they will react remains to be seen.

That many of the modern weapon systems mentioned in this study are about to enter service is beyond doubt. As they do so, Israel should be able to dismantle as much as one-quarter to one-third of its enormous, industrial-age ground forces with their sixteen or so divisions.[21] To gain an impression of what that means, take the U.S. as the only superpower with commitments all over the globe; yet somehow it gets along with only twelve (including two Marine Corps) divisions plus a few of the National Guard. Even disregarding the manpower costs—most of the forces consist of reservists who are only called up in an emergency and receive their pay by means of Social Security—the savings that scrapping thousands upon thousands of vehicles and the maintenance services they require can bring about are tremendous. This is all the more so because many of them are now so worn out that they require constant attention and will barely start. For example, the last time the IDF purchased large numbers of tank transporters was during the years of rapid expansion that followed the 1973 War; the same applies to armored fighting vehicles, artillery barrels, and many other kinds of equipment. Some of the tanks are real antiques, having entered service either before or immediately after 1967 and taken part in every war and skirmish since then. Over time they have been subject to so many repairs, upgrades, and modifications as to resemble not so much fighting machines as rolling junkyards; imagine what Hertz Rent a Car would look like if it tried to run a fleet of cars that old.

As part of a long-overdue reform, the command structure of the IDF will be flattened, decentralized, and networked.[22] The remaining formations should be reshaped into brigade-sized, mobile, battle teams. The teams will integrate ground forces, attack helicopters, and assault helicopters capable of lifting special forces to the places where they may be needed at the time they are needed; see, by way of an example, the operations of the U.S. 101st Division in Iraq. Each group will come complete with up-to-date means of intelligence such as UAVs, sensors of the kind described above, and computerized war rooms capable of gathering and making use of the data they gather. As was already the case with the Americans in Iraq, each will be able to call on air support when needed and obtain it very quickly. Instead of their present-day organic services, which will be dismantled, they will be backed by a modern logistic infrastructure that makes better use of the possibilities provided by the RMA.[23] As a result, tactically they will be much more mobile than present forces are; swarming around any would-be invader like a pack of wolves on their prey, attacking where they can and carrying out temporary retreats where they must. Since responsibility for the logistic infrastructure will be shifted from the units to the fronts, these changes will also make them much easier to move from one front to another. Which, given Israel's geographic position amidst its enemies, is a critically important requirement.

Concerning armament, one possibility would be to build the new units around the Merkava IV tank, which entered production in 2001 and which, in some respects, is the world's most advanced.[24] Another, and perhaps better, option would be to forget about tanks altogether, stopping or limiting the production of Merkavas and proceeding straight to the next generation of light, high-mobility, missile-firing armored vehicles now on the drawing board in several countries.[25] These reforms, plus a navy with considerably expanded sea-to-shore capabilities, may finally permit Israel to join most other developed countries by abolishing conscription. Another possibility would be to institute some form of selective service; various ways of carrying out the change are being considered even now.[26] In terms of both materiel and personnel, the overriding objective should be to pit quality against quantity. Since the former and not the latter has always been Israel's forte, such a change can only work to its advantage.

What is true in military, economic, and social terms is even more true for technology in general. Technological superiority is most useful in winning an armed conflict when that conflict is waged in a simple environment—outer space, for example, or the earth's atmosphere. It is there, and there alone, that the absence of clutter of any kind permits sensors to function without interference; any blip that appears on a screen represents a target, and unless it responds to IFF interrogation any target can be shot at. Not only are there fewer false alarms, but the power of weapons may be maximized without fear of doing so much collateral damage that the outcome may be counterproductive. All this explains why warfare in these environments was the first to be partly automated, as with many ground-to-air and sea-to-air defense systems.[27]

At the other extreme, the entire history of guerrilla warfare suggests that, the more complex the environment, the less important the role technological superiority can play and the greater that of other factors. One of them is numbers, though in guerrilla warfare that has seldom been decisive since "the forces of order" greatly outnumbered the active combatants on the other side. Others are popular support—guerrillas, as Mao Tze Dong said, must have a sea to swim in—organization, training, doctrine, and leadership. Perhaps most important of all are motivation and the readiness to fight to the death if necessary. As numerous suicide bombings demonstrate, these are precisely the fields where Israel's enemies hold their strongest cards; and no wonder, given that they have little but their shackles to lose. Israel's own experience proves that shooting down a real cruise missile may be easier than intercepting a human one in the form of a suicide bomber. The same experience shows that building an antimissile system may be more feasible than stopping the primitive Al Kassam rockets that continue to be fired from Gaza whenever the Palestinians feel in the mood and which, in the future, will no doubt be fired in and from the West Bank as well. Not the least advantage of reconstructing Israel's defense along the lines here discussed is that technology will be pulled out of the clutter that smothers it, so to speak, and given a free rein to show what it can do. Once this is done, the country will be able to capitalize on its advantages rather than throwing many of them away, as it does at present. To put the idea in economic terms, Israel will be back in a position where it can maximize its comparative advantage. For which, given the critical situation in which it finds itself, it is high time.

To sum up, Israel today is like a man who has stepped on a caltrop and one of whose legs has become gangrenous as a result. Since he insisted on standing on the caltrop, the infection spread and it is now threatening to kill him. So far, however, all he has been doing is to try and affect a cure; either administering antibiotics or, when that did not work, beating the leg and calling it bad names for refusing to heal. What is needed, of course, is to apply a tourniquet and amputate. Either this is done, or the patient will die.

Ever since Israel gained its independence, perhaps the most fundamental assumption underlying its defense has been that terrorism represents mere pinpricks. Though occasionally expensive, and certainly unpleasant for those involved, if necessary it could be coped with forever; meanwhile the country's "basic" security could only be put at risk by the neighboring Arab states with their tanks, aircraft, and, increasingly, weapons of mass destruction and their delivery vehicles. Both before and after 1967, Israel's entire strategy, specifically including the concept of "defensible borders" itself, grew directly from these ideas. So did the structure of its fighting forces. This includes not just the balance between the arms and services but the reserve system, the command and control system, the priority given or not given to the regional commands, the relationship between offense and defense, and much else.

As we saw, the conventional threat is rapidly becoming out of date if, indeed, it has not disappeared already. In the Middle East and elsewhere hordes of tanks, the artillery and mechanized infantry that accompany them, and the vast rear services that support them are going out of fashion much in the same way as those tanks themselves replaced the infantry forces of World War I. In part, the decline of conventional warfare is due to the fact that any country that can build forces capable of waging it can also develop nuclear weapons, borrow them, or steal them. As Allon, for his own reasons, foresaw decades ago, the resulting balance of terror also applies to the Middle East; it, too, is following where the rest of the world leads. In part it is because, even if the forces *can* defeat their opposite numbers and capture territory, as exemplified most recently by the Americans in Iraq, they are going to have a very difficult time coping with the terrorism that inevitably follows. All this must be considered against the fact that, both in world terms and compared to those of Israel, the combined Arab armed forces are now far weaker than at any time since the June 1967 War showed an astonished world what the IDF could do. The enemy state which, from about 1980 on, was the strongest of all, has simply ceased to exist. Of the rest, one major opponent has been left behind for technical and economic reasons, whereas another has been at peace with Israel for twenty years. Are we dreaming, or is it real?

To look at it in another way, at present most of the Arab states may be divided into two classes. Those that are rich and willing to undertake at least some steps towards social and political modernization tend to be small and far away from Israel, as Kuwait, Qatar, and the Emirates are. Those that are fairly large and close at hand, such as Egypt and Syria, also tend to be poor and backward. The social systems of the countries in question owe more to the concentration camp and the execution wall than to free discussion, democratic elections, and an independent judiciary capable of safeguarding human rights. For this and other reasons, they are less capable of providing a sound basis for building and maintaining future military power than was the case during the age of large-scale Arab-Israeli wars. It is true that the Arab armed forces, the Egyptian ones in particular, have done what they could to recruit young people with a reasonable education. On the other hand, there are indications that their efforts in this direction have not always been as successful as they might have wished,[1] a fact which is all the more important because skills in such vital fields as programming computers and operating data-links are best acquired almost from birth on.

While the conventional threat has been receding and may, perhaps, never be rebuilt, the one presented by WMDs is alive and well. Both in and outside Israel, some people would argue that it is steadily growing as countries in the region try to acquire the weapons and/or perfect their delivery vehicles and add more of them to their arsenals.[2] With Iraq taken out of the picture for a long time, perhaps forever, Prime Minister Sharon claims that the greatest danger is presented by Iran;[3] are we to understand this to mean that, within a radius of 900 miles from Tel Aviv, there is no serious threat left? Be the answer to this question as it may, almost a decade and a half's worth of forecasts concerning the date when Tehran might obtain the bomb have proved false. Worse still, the American failure to find WMDs in Iraq has put both the capabilities of some intelligence services and their honesty under a cloud.[4] The information they spread may be as slanted in the one case as it was in the other. In fact, there is reason to think that, in the past, some of them have exaggerated the Iranian effort. This is true both in regard to the weapons themselves and in respect to the delivery vehicles needed to carry them, which were supposed to become operational much earlier than actually proved the case.[5] Nor should this be reason for surprise. Some of the information the services peddled apparently originated in the Mujahedin Khalk, a terrorist group whose goal is to overthrow the government in Tehran and which at one time received support from Saddam Hussein.[6] Even if we accept that the threat of missiles and WMDs *is* growing, and even if the worst possible scenarios are considered, then coping with it has little if anything to do with whether Israel does, or does not, maintain control over the Territories.

As then Prime Minister Rabin was among the first to recognize,[7] while these changes are going on, escalating terrorism is rapidly turning into a matter of life and death. This is less because of the direct damage that terrorists can inflict, which in spite of everything has been kept within fairly narrow limits, than because of their impact on Israeli society and, in particular, the million-plus strong Arab minority within the country's borders. Less so in the immediate term than some years hence when, unless a miracle happens and Jews start multiplying as fishes used to do, they are bound to become a diminishing minority between the Mediterranean and the Jordan River. To quote President George W. Bush, speaking of the *Intifada* in the autumn of 2001, when bombs were going off almost every day: "In the Holy Land, the future itself is being assassinated." On pain of that future looking black indeed, it is imperative to put an end to the present situation as soon as possible. And do so, of course, in a manner that does not jeopardize the existence of the Jewish State in other ways.

Given the geographic and demographic realities as spelled out in the present volume, clearly defending a Territories-less Israel will be neither easy nor cheap. It will require some highly innovative solutions that will challenge the ingenuity of the country's political leaders, armed forces, defense industries, and scientists. On the other hand, $20 billion lost to the Palestinian Uprising represents an awful lot of money even for states much larger and richer than Israel. Even if one only calculates the direct military outlay (about $6 billion), then a fraction of that sum, invested in RMA-type technology as it ought to have been, would have permitted very considerable progress to be made. And this is to say nothing about the sums wasted to put settlers into Territories where, as even some of those responsible for Israel's defense admit, they can do nobody and nothing any good at all. And from which, sooner or later, a very considerable number will have to be evacuated and resettled for the second time.

Of the various technical possibilities considered above, few if any are entirely original. Although a number of them are still some years away and others may not be selected for further development, not one belongs to the realm of science fiction or is impossible in principle. Practically all have been discussed both abroad and in Israel itself; among the Israelis who discussed them were some of the country's highest ranking, and intellectually most respected, defense experts, officers, and scientists. Partly because it is assisted by the U.S.A., partly owing to its own resources, Israel is better positioned than most countries—a fortiori, than any other Middle Eastern country—to develop, deploy, and operate the systems in question. The necessary research and development facilities, which take years if not decades to build, are already in place. As the list of the countries to which they export their wares suggests, they are world-famous for their advanced capabilities. From Tokyo to Rome and from the Ural Mountains to South Africa there is nothing like them. Indeed, one can hardly open an issue of the relevant literature without coming across a reference to Israel R.&D. and its products.

Many of the component parts are also readily available. Instead of having to be developed from scratch, they only have be adapted to each other and to new launching platforms. Probably the most difficult job of all is designing the appropriate command, control, and communications systems. Fortunately, though, that is precisely Israel's forte; few other countries have such an abundant supply of both the necessary manpower and the creativity the task demands. With some luck Israel should be able to export those systems, or parts of them, to other countries, thus spreading the cost of research and development while also earning badly needed foreign currency. This applies in particular to missiles, UAVs, UCAVs, and every kind of electronic equipment from avionics and radar to laser range finders and night vision devices. In the past many governments, fearing the power of the Arab states as well as bad public relations inside their own countries, were reluctant to buy major weapon systems such as tanks and combat aircraft simply because they bore the label "made in Israel."[8] Thanks partly to the growth of Israel's own economy, partly to the discovery of new oil reserves all over the world, those days are mostly gone. Moreover, this factor is much less likely to affect the sale of the smaller, less visible items we are talking of here; if Indonesia buys Israeli mini-UAVs, few people are going to object. In this way, as in so many others, the Revolution in Military Affairs represents the right thing at the right time for Israel. Had it not existed, it would need to be invented.

Most important of all, the above analysis, however brief, suggests that such a defense is no more impossible now than it was before 1967. In part, this is because of advances in military technology. Those advances are rapidly giving the advantage to firepower, taking it away from the maneuvers on which any attacker must necessarily rely and making it possible to identify his main force and deal with it. They are, indeed, likely to prevent him from concentrating in the first place; what will happen to a force that tries to do so nevertheless was demonstrated, perhaps for the last time, back in 1991 when the Iraqi attempt to organize a counterattack at Khafji was quickly discovered and repulsed. Underlying these changes are shifts in the balance of power which, reflecting the economic trends of two decades, has decisively swung in Israel's favor. With Saddam gone, the shift has become even more pronounced. This in turn affects the position of Syria and any other Arab country, such as Egypt, that might one day take it into its head to renew the war with Israel. Unable to recover the Golan Heights by force, an operation which does not appear feasible at present, Damascus may yet decide on peace, and indeed in the summer of 2003 Bashir Assad indicated his willingness to resume the talks from the point where Rabin left them. If not, then this situation should present Israel with no very great difficulty; no greater, at any rate, than has been the case since at least 1982.

A unilateral Israeli withdrawal from the Territories will leave some problems unsolved.[9] Probably the most important is that of the Palestinian refugees, who are said to number between four and five million, worldwide.[10] Ever since the question was first created in 1948, the Arab states have often used the Right of Return as a battering ram against

Israel, and any future Palestinian Government may well do the same. Even if it does not, it may well be powerless to make its people renounce that Right in their hearts; one reason why most Palestinians oppose the wall even now is precisely because it threatens to end any possibility of exercising it. Everything considered, it is doubtful whether, short of committing suicide, there is *anything* Israel can do to solve that problem in a way that will really give the other side satisfaction, let alone prevent it from raising its head in the future. A withdrawal will also lead to new problems, such as control over water resources, which this study does not address.[11]

Concerning the refugees, a Palestinian State in the West Bank and the Gaza Strip, for all its shortcomings, will at least provide a place where some of them can go. Another advantage would be that Arab Israelis can be dispatched there in case they continue to cause trouble; for the rest, one can only hope that time will cause the number of refugees who want to return to diminish until there are few left at all. Concerning water, a hint towards an answer may perhaps be found in the fact that, even today, Israel exports desalination plants to numerous countries all over the world. The one Israeli city that has no water shortage, Eilat, is entirely dependent on such a plant;[12] yet paradoxically tourism, on which Eilat lives, is a "thirsty" industry. Of the annual amount of water Israel needs, 1,800 million cubic meters, only about 450 million come from the West Bank. Hence desalination and recycling might present acceptable alternatives. By one calculation recycling alone could yield another 350 million cubic meters a year as early as 2020.[13] Add another 100 million from a desalination plant presently under construction and, on paper at any rate, the problem is solved; this, without considering the substitution of effluent for potable water in agriculture (saving 350 million cubic meters)[14] and the possible use of emerging methods such as nano-technology. By way of a final word on these issues, it should be said that their complexity, the links between them, and the influence of uncontrollable outside forces makes it impossible to foresee all the implications. As Churchill, preparing to order some new Dreadnoughts in his capacity as Lord of the Admiralty, wrote in 1912, thought bifurcates too fast. Had he waited for all possibilities to be explored before deciding, then the ships would still be on the drawing board.

Rather than try to do the impossible, this study will end by pointing out that Israel has no choice. Either it builds an iron wall[15] and rids itself of what Moshe Dayan once called "the blemish of conquest"[16]— even Ariel Sharon, in his more conciliatory moments, agrees or at least says he agrees there simply is no other way—or else it can have no future. As the deterioration in its situation since October 2000 shows only too clearly, the longer it waits the worse the problem is likely to become, to say nothing of the terrible human suffering caused by the continuing bloodshed on both sides. Mutatis mutandis, what the Book of Exodus has to say about the Israelites in Egypt now applies to the Palestinian People in the Territories. "The more they were oppressed, the faster they multiplied and burst their dams." In the struggle between Jewish guns and Palestinian wombs it is the latter and not the former that is bound to prevail; the more so because, so long as the Uprising goes on, Jewish immigration is bound to remain limited. As to what Israel should do, the command of Deuteronomy is even more imperious:

> Lo I set before thee today life and the good, death and evil . . . and thou shalt choose the good . . . so that thou and thine offspring mayest live . . . in the country that God the Lord has sworn unto thine fathers Abraham and Yitzhak and Jakob to give unto thee.

INTRODUCTION

1. For some attempts to measure the intensity of the conflict see H. Ben-Yehuda and S. Sandler, *The Arab-Israeli Conflict Transformed,* New York, NY, State University of New York Press, 2002, pp. 31–2 (table 2.1), 60–1 (table 3.1), 87 (table 4.1), 89 (table 4.2), 90 (table 4.3), 91 (table 4.3), 92 (table 4.5), 93 (table 4.6), 96–7 (table 4.7), 135–6 (table 5.3).

2. On the way many Arabs perceive U.S. involvement in the conflict see B. J. Talbot and M. B. Meyer, "View from the East: Arab Perceptions of United States Presence and Policy", INSS Occasional Paper 48, Colorado Springs, CO, USAF Academy, 2003, pp. 3–11.

3. Israel Business Data Survey, quoted in *Yediot Achronot* [Hebrew], 10 June 2003, p. 16.

4. See on this Y. Peri, "The Israeli Military and Israel's Palestinian Policy: From Oslo to the Al Aqsa Intifada", *Peaceworks,* No. 47, Washington, D.C., U.S. Institute of Peace, Washington, D.C., 2002; also Y. Levy, *The Other Army of Israel* [Hebrew], Tel Aviv, Yediot Achronot, 2003, p. 398.

5. Research by Dr. R. Melnik as reported in *Yediot Achronot* Weekend Magazine, 29.11.2002, pp. 12–3; *Maariv* Finance [Hebrew], 9 June 2003, p. 3; *Yediot Achronot.* 23 June 2003, p. 11.

6. Talk to the Washington Institute of Middle East Studies, reported on Israel Radio, 1.12.2002.

7. The IDF did, however, allow a short version of this book to appear in the May 2003 issue of its flagship publication, *Maarachot* [Hebrew].

1. ISRAELI DEFENSE BEFORE 1967

1. See on this E. Efrat, *Geography of Occupation; Judea, Samaria and the Gaza Strip* [Hebrew], Jerusalem, Carmel, 2002, pp. 23–4.

2. For a blow by blow of this episode see M. B. Oren, *Six Days of War,* New York, NY, Oxford University Press, 2002, pp. 31–5.

3. There is a detailed analysis of the raid in A. Ayalon, "Operation Shredder", *Maarachot,* 261/262, March-April 1978, pp. 27–38.

4. See H. Bartov, *Dado: Forty-Eight Years and Twenty Days* [Hebrew], Tel Aviv, Maariv, 1978, pp. 126–9.

5. See H. Laskov, "The Origins of Doctrine, 1949–50" [Hebrew], *Maarachot,* No. 191/192, 1968; A. Levite, *Offense and Defense in Israel's Military Doctrine,* Boulder,

CO, 1989, chapter 2; and M. van Creveld, *The Sword and the Olive; A Critical History of the Israel Defense Force,* New York, NY, 1998, pp. 105–6, 157–63.

6. According to S. Golan, *Hot Border, Cold War* [Hebrew], Tel Aviv, Maarachot, 2000, pp. 225, 229.

7. M. Gur, "The Experiences of Sinai", *Maarachot,* October 1966, p. 18.

8. The best source is A. Adan, "Quality and Quantity in the Yom Kippur War", in A. Kover, ed., *Quality and Quantity* [Hebrew], Tel Aviv, *Ministry of Defense,* 1985, p. 257, tables 1 and 2.

9. Its development is described in D. Shalom, *Like a Bolt Out of the Blue: "Moked" Operation in the Six Day War* [Hebrew], Rishon Lezion, Baavir, 2002.

10. See on this T. N. Dupuy, *Numbers, Predictions, and War; Using History to Evaluate Combat Factors and Predict the Outcome of Battles,* New York, NY, Bobbs-Merill, 1979, p. 133.

11. E. G. D. Ben Gurion, *A Special Destiny: Essays on Israel's Defense,* [Hebrew], Tel Aviv, Maarachot, 1971, p. 129.

12. On the early history of the Israeli bomb see most recently A. Cohen, *Israel and the Bomb,* New York, NY, Columbia University Press, 1998, pp. 41–56.

13. M. Mardor, *Rafael: Research and Development for Israel's Defense,* Tel Aviv, Ministry of Defense, 1981 [Hebrew], pp. 498–9, has a veiled description of the weapons being assembled.

2. THE BIRTH OF "DEFENSIBLE BORDERS"

1. See R. Pedatzur, "Evolving Ballistic Missile Capabilities and Theater Missile Defense: The Israeli Predicament", *Security Studies,* 3, 3, 1994, pp. 531–70.

2. See on this D. Horowitz, "Israel's Concept of Defensible Borders", *Jerusalem Papers on Peace Problems,* Jerusalem, Leonard Davis Institute of International Relations, No. 16, 1975, p. 5.

3. See on this W. Bass, *Support Any Friend; Kennedy's Middle East and the Making of the U.S.–Israeli Alliance,* New York, NY, Oxford University Press, 2003, pp. 20, 42, 43, 48, 50, 57, 75, 148, 155.

4. See on this episode U. Ben Yosef, *The Best of Enemies: Israel and Transjordan in the War of 1948,* London, Cass, 1987, pp. 206–13; also I. Pappe, *Britain and the Arab-Israeli Conflict, 1948–1951,* New York, N.Y., St. Martin's Press, 1988, pp. 18–82.

5. Quote from M. Bar On, *Smoking Borders,* Jerusalem, Yad Ben Tzvi, 2001, p 136.

6. Y. Rabin, *Service Record* [Hebrew], Tel Aviv, 1979, vol. i, p. 150.

7. The map, which gives Israel much of the Golan Heights, much of the West Bank, the Gaza Strip, a piece of Sinai near Elath, and another near the Straits of Tiran, is reproduced in E. Sohar, *A Concubine in the Middle East: American-Israeli Relations,* Jerusalem, Ariel, 1999, p. 40. See also <http://search.yahoo.com/search?p=Israel+defensible+borders&vm=i&n=20&fl=0&x=wrt>.

8. See M. Dayan, *Story of My Life*, London, 1976, pp. 91–6.

9. See most recently M. Mayzel, *The Golan Heights Campaign*, June 1967 [Hebrew], Tel Aviv, Ministry of Defense, 2001, p. 248 ff.; also Oren, *Six Days of War*, p. 229.

10. *A Curtain of Sand* [Hebrew], Tel Aviv, Hakibbutz Hameuchad, 1958.

11. Quoted in A. Busheri, "The Security Concept of Yigal Allon as Compared to that of Ben Gurion" [Hebrew], PhD. Thesis submitted to the Hebrew University, Jerusalem 2003, p. 197.

12. R. Tal, "Dayan—A Recokning", *Yediot Achronot*, 27 April 1997.

13. See Y. Allon, "Israel: The Case for Defensible Borders", *Foreign Affairs*, 55, 1, October 1976, pp. 37–53. In addition to the Jordan Valley and parts of the Golan Heights, Allon also wanted to retain small parts of the Sinai.

14. See on this van Creveld, *The Sword and the Olive*, pp. 201–2.

15. According to Oren, *Six Days of War*, p. 277.

16. G. Meir, *My Life*, Jerusalem, Steimatzky, 1975, pp. 356–7.

17. Pedatzur, *The Triumph of Embarrassment*, p. 224.

18. See van Creveld, *The Sword and the Olive*, pp. 5–14.

19. See on this van Creveld, *The Sword and the Olive*, pp. 106–7.

20. A. Braun, *Moshe Dayan In the Yom Kippur War* [Hebrew], Tel Aviv, Idanim, 1993, p. 97.

21. E.g. future Minister of Defense Moshe Arens, Lecture at Tel Aviv University, 2 March 1978; in Jafee Center for Strategic Studies, ed., "Secure Borders; Proceedings of a Panel Discussion", Tel Aviv, Tel Aviv University, 1978, p. 36.

22. Out of about 100 settlements 75 have fewer than 1,000 inhabitants; Efrat, *Geography of Occupation*, pp. 57 (map 9), 58, 59.

23. Lecture at Tel Aviv University, 2 March 1978; in Jafee Center for Strategic Studies, ed., "Secure Borders", p. 9.

24. Lecture at Tel Aviv University, 2 March 1978; in Jafee Center for Strategic Studies, ed., "Secure Borders", pp. 12–4.

25. E. Weizman, *The Battle for Peace* [Hebrew], Jerusalem, Idanim, 1982, pp. 133–4.

26. For some figures see The International Institute of Strategic Studies, *The Military Balance*, London, IISS, 1973–4 and 1980–1.

27. *Maariv* [Hebrew], 18 February 1982, p. 2.

28. On Israel's fears in this regard see Weizman, *The Battle for Peace*, p. 152.

29. Data from Y. Lifshitz, "The Economics of Defense: Theory and the Israeli Case" [Hebrew], Jerusalem, Jerusalem Institute, 2000, p. 170.

30. See E. Dowek, *Israeli-Egyptian Relations, 1980-2000*, London, Cass, 2001, pp. 246–7.

31. *The Battle for Peace*, p. 202.

32. A. Arian, *Security Threatened: Surveying Israeli Opinion on Peace and War*, Cambridge, Cambridge University Press, 1995, pp. 102–3, tables 4.3, 4.4, 4.5, 4.6, have some interesting figures on this question.

33. See F. Mehring, *Karl Marx, Geschichte seinies Lebens*, Leipzig, Soziologisch Verlagsanstalt, 1933, pp. 487–8.

3. THE GRAND STRATEGIC EQUATION

1. A good summary of these problems is Y. Rabin, "Deterrence in an Israeli Security Context", in A. Kleiman and A. Levite, eds., *Deterrence in the Middle East: Where Theory and Practice Converge*, Tel Aviv, Jafee Center for Strategic Studies, 1993, pp. 7–9.

2. See on this A. Kapur, "Nuclear Policies of Small States and Weaker Powers", in E. Inbar and G. Sheffer, eds., *The National Security of Small States in a Changing World*, London, Cass, 1997, pp. 107–8.

3. See on this P. R. Kumarsawamy, "India and Israel: Evolving Strategic Relationship", *Mideast Security and Policy Studies*, No. 40, Ramat Gan, Begin-Sadat Center for Strategic Studies, 1998.

4. See on this U. Bialer, *Between East and West: Israeli Foreign Orientation, 1948–1956*, Cambridge, Cambridge University Press, 1990.

5. See, for details, M. Bar On, *The Gates of Gaza*, New York, NY, St. Martin's Press, 1994, pp. 1–15.

6. See on this S. D. Rodman, "War Initiation: The Case of Israel", *Journal of Strategic Studies*, 20, 4, December 1997, pp. 10–1.

7. See on this E. Karsh, *The Cautious Bear: Soviet Military Engagement in the Middle East Wars since 1967*, Boulder, CO, Westview, 1985; also T. Friedgut, "The Soviet Union in the Middle East", in I. Stockman-Shomron, ed., Israel, *The Middle East and the Great Powers*, Jerusalem, Shikmona, 1984, p. 112.

8. According to E. Wald, *The Wald Report: The Decline of Israel's National Security*, Boulder, CO, Westview Press, 1992, pp. 45–6.

9. See Oren, *Six Days of War*, p. 297.

10. See on this topic O. Antonenko, "Russian Military Involvement in the Middle East since 1990", *Maarachot*, 378–79, November 2001, pp, 36–45.

11. For an analysis of past U.S. behavior in this respect, see G. L. Sorokin, "Patrons, Clients, and Allies in the Arab-Israeli Conflict", *Journal of Strategic Studies*, 20, 1, March 1997, pp. 63–7.

12. See on these events Oren, *Six Days of War*, pp. 71–170.

13. *Service Record*, vol. I pp. 262–64.

14. For the details see A. El Edroos, *The Hashemite Arab Army 1909–1979*, Amman, The Publishing Committee, pp. 449–60; M. Zak, *Hussein Makes Peace* [Hebrew], Ramat Gan, Bar Illan University Press, 1996, pp. 141–2.

15. Murhaf Jouejati, Syrian political analyst, in R. B. Parker, ed., *The October War: A Retroperspective,* Gainsville, FL, University Press of Florida, 2001, pp. 103, 120.

16. See on this episode G. Golan, "The Soviet Union and the Yom Kippur War", in P. R. Kumaraswamy, ed., *Revisiting the Yom Kippur War,* London, Cass, 2000, pp. 143–6; also, from a somewhat different perspective, A. Summer, *The Arrogance of Power: The Secret World of Richard Nixon,* London, Phoenix, 2000, pp. 459–62.

17. See, in respect to Iraq, S. Nakdimon, *Tammuz in Flames* [Hebrew], Jerusalem, Idanim, 1993, pp. 285–6; and, in respect to Lebanon, Z. Schiff, "Green Light, Lebanon", *Foreign Policy,* 50, spring 1983, pp. 73–85.

18. See on this C. Lipson, "American Support for Israel: History, Sources, Limits", in G. Sheffer, ed., *U.S.-Israeli Relations at the Crossroads,* London, Cass, 1997, pp. 128–46.

19. For a short account see G. M. Steinberg, "Israel and the United States: Can the Special Relationship Survive the New Strategic Environment?" in B. Rubin and Th. Kearney, eds., *U.S. Allies in a Changing World,* London, Cass, 2001, pp. 135–80.

20. On the history of the American-Israeli nuclear "compact" see Bass, *Support Any Friend,* pp. 186–238; on the means used to turn the Dimona inspections into a farce, Cohen, *Israel and the Bomb,* pp. 175–85.

21. For this story see S. M. Hersch, *The Samson Option; Israel's Nuclear Arsenal and American Foreign Policy,* New York, NY, Random House, 1991, pp. 271–84.

22. See on this Sohar, *A Concubine in the Middle East,* pp. 171–8.

23. See on Christian-American support for Israel K. D. Wald and others, "Reclaiming Zion: How American Religious Groups View the Middle East", in Sheffer, ed., *U.S.-Israeli Relations at the Crossroads,* pp. 147–69.

24. See <http://www.analisidifesa.it/numero6/eng/falconeng.htm>.

25. A. Eban, *The New Diplomacy: International Affairs in the Modern Age,* New York, NY, Random House, 1983, p. 218.

26. *Haaretz,* 3 December 1974; E. Inbar, "Yitzhak Rabin and Israel's National Security", *Journal of Strategic Studies,* 20, 2, June 1997, p. 28.

27. Quoted in E. Kafkafi, *Pinhas Lavon—Anti Messiah,* a Biography [Hebrew], Tel Aviv, Am Oved, 1998, p. 231.

28. M. Dayan, *Shall the Sword Devour Forever?* [Hebrew], Tel Aviv, Idanim, 1981, p. 117.

29. Israel Radio News Bulletin, 23 June 2003.

30. See on this, most recently, A. Fishman, "The IDF Plans a Return to a Preventive Strike", *Yediot Achronot,* Weekend Magazine, 16 May 2003, pp. 8–9.

4. DEFENDING AGAINST TERRORISM

1. E. A. Cohen and others, eds., *Knives, Tanks and Missiles,* Washington, D.C., Washington Institute for Near East Policy, 1998.

2. *The Transformation of War,* New York, NY, Free Press, 1991, particularly chapters 1 and 7; also *The Rise and Fall of the State,* London, Cambridge University Press, 1999, pp. 337–54.

3. C. J. Gross, *American Military Aviation: The Indispensable Arm,* College Station, TX, Texas A&M University Press, 2000, p. 290.

4. Quoted in Oren, *Six Days of War,* p. 253.

5. J. Alsop, "Moshe Dayan's Motto", *Washington Post,* 8.12.1967.

6. The quote is from *Yediot Achronot,* "The Shock of the Territories", Special Supplement, 14 January 1988.

7. See most recently D. A. Charles, "Eyes of the Underground: Jewish Insurgent Intelligence in Palestine, 1945–47", *Intelligence and National Security,* 13, 4, winter 1998, especially pp. 172–5.

8. See on this, most recently, C. Jones, " 'A Reach Greater than the Grasp'; Israeli Intelligence and the Conflict in Southern Lebanon", *Intelligence and National Security,* 16, 3, autumn 2002, pp. 1–26; also Peri, "The Israeli Military", p. 31.

9. See, for the details, *International Defense Review,* 9/1995, pp. 73–4.

10. Dr. D. Sobelman, Tel Aviv University, quoting Lebanese papers, Israel TV News Bulletin, 10 August 2003.

11. General (ret.) Matan Vilnai, Israel TV evening news bulletin, 13 November 2002. On 29 June 2003 the assertion was repeated by former Prime Minister Benjamin Netanyahu; Israel Radio News Bulletin.

12. Radio Israel News Bulletin, 9 June 2003.

13. Interview in *Yediot Achronot,* Weekend Magazine, 11 April 2003, p. 6.

14. Radio Israel News Bulletin, 9 March 2003.

15. For some of what is available see <http://www.magal-ssl.com/pages/products.asp>.

16. Maps of one such scheme may be found in S. L. Gordon, *Israel Against Terror: A National Assessment* [Hebrew], n.p, Melzer, 2002, pp. 146–7.

17. Figures from Efrat, *Geography of Occupation,* p. 195.

18. According to IDF Intelligence Chief General Amos Malka, *Yediot Achronot,* Holiday Supplement, 26 September 2001, p. 2.

19. S. L. Gordon, "Dimensions of Quality: A New Approach to Net Assessment of Airpower", JFSS Memorandum No. 64, Tel Aviv, Jafee Center for Strategic Studies, 2003, p. 59 fig. 5.

20. Interview with Ehud Barak, *Yediot Achronot,* Weekend Magazine, 11 April 2003, p. 6; G. Leshem and E. Glickman, "Laughing All the way to the Fence", *Yediot Achronot,* Weekend Magazine, 11 April 2003, pp. 20–1, 24; S. Plotzker, "The Economic Crisis Has Won", *Yediot Achronot,* Weekend Magazine, 5 June 2003, p. 5.

21. See on this C. R. Shrader, *The First Helicopter War: Logistics and Mobility in Algeria, 1954–1962,* Westport, CT, Praeger, 1999, pp. 208–9.

22. S. Plotzker, "The Economic Crisis Has Won", *Yediot Achronot,* Weekend Magazine, 5 June 2003, p. 5.

23. See, most recently, M. Barnea, "The Charities of the Islamic Movement", *Yediot Achronot,* Weekend Magazine, 5 June 2003, pp. 2–3.

24. Israel TV, news bulletin, 14 July 2003.

25. See on this, most recently, interview with General (ret.) Ami Ayalon, former head of Israel's Security Service, in *Yediot Achronot,* Weekend Magazine, pp. 6–7.

26. See on this Efrat, *Geography of Occupation,* pp. 93, 98–102; also the maps in M. Rapoport, "Four Maps and a Golden Solution", *Yediot Achronot,* Weekend Supplement, 27 June 2003, pp. 22–3.

27. Figures from Efrat, *Geography of Occupation,* p. 136.

5. DEALING WITH CONVENTIONAL WARFARE

1. Figures from I. Ben Israel, "Security, Technology and the Future Battlefield", in H. Golan, ed., *Israel's Security Web: Core Issues of Israel's National Security in Its Sixth Decade* [Hebrew], Tel Aviv, Maarachot, 2001, p. 287.

2. See on this A. Oren, "The Geographer in the Service of Military Planning in Israel", *Maarachot,* 385, September 2002, p. 60.

3. See, for some of the details, Sohar, *A Concubine in the Middle East,* pp. 152–3.

4. Brom and Shapir, *The Middle East Military Balance,* pp. 125, 179–83.

5. See on this B. Lewis, *What Went Wrong? Western Impact and Middle Eastern Response,* New York, NY, Phoenix, 2002.

6. 1995 figures: Ben Israel, "Security, Technology and the Future Battlefield", p. 297.

7. In Israel there is now one mobile for every two persons. Arab figures from H. T. Azzam, *The Arab World Facing the Challenge of the New Millennium,* London, Tauris, 2002, p. 43 table 45.

8. All figures from Brom and Shapir, *The Middle East Military Balance,* pp. 177 (Israel), 313 (Syria), 197 (Jordan), 123 (Egypt), and 288 (Saudi Arabia).

9. Gordon, "Dimensions of Quality", p. 59 fig. 5.

10. This point, interestingly enough, was already being made in the mid-1970s; see Y. Evron, "The Demilitarization of the Middle East and Arms Control", [Hebrew], in *Towards Alternative Solutions to the Israel-Arab Conflict,* Jerusalem, The Van Leer Foundation, ed., 1974, p. 21.

11. On the developing Israeli-Turkish relationship see E. Inbar, "The Israeli-Turkish Strategic Relationship", *Turkish Studies,* 3, 2, autumn 2002, especially pp. 24–7, 29; also O. Bengio and G. Ozcan, "Arab Perceptions of Turkey and its Alignment with Israel", *Mideast Security and Policy Studies,* No. 48, Ramat Gan, Begin-Sadat Center for Strategic Studies, 2001.

12. *Haaretz* [Hebrew], 3 June 1997.

13. E. Inbar and S. Sandler, "Israel's Deterrence Strategy Revisited", *Security Studies*, 3, 2, winter 1993–94, p. 334. A good comparison of Syria's armed forces with those of Israel, valid for 1991, is available in A. Shalev, *Israel and Syria: Peace and Security on the Golan* [Hebrew], Tel Aviv, Tel Aviv University, 1991, p. 125.

14. Gordon, "Dimensions of Quality", p. 60 figure 7.

15. According to Antonenko, "Russian Military Involvement in the Middle East since 1990", p. 41.

16. See on this Y. Klein, "Russian Arms Transfer Policy and the Middle East", in E. Inbar and S. Sandler, eds., *Middle Eastern Security Prospects for an Arms Control Regime*, London, Cass, 1995, pp. 34–48.

17. ACDA data available at <http://dostan.lib.vit.edu/acda/wmeat97/mks_trd.pdf>. The ACDA data do not include the $2 billion that Israel got from the U.S. in this year, and which I have added on my own.

18. Interview with General (ret.) Uri Saguy, *Yediot Achronot*, Weekend Magazine, 18 April 2003. There is a more extended discussion of the Israeli-Syrian balance of forces in U. Saguy, "The Strategic Significance of the Change in the Syrian Position", in M. Maoz, ed., *The Golan Between War and Peace* [Hebrew], Or Yehuda, 1999, pp. 148–9.

19. An Iraqi brigade did, however, enter Jordan at the time; see S. Shai, "The Suez Campaign and the Fear of Iraqi Intervention", in S. Shai, ed., *The Iraqi-Israeli Conflict 1948–2000* [Hebrew], Tel Aviv, Ministry of Defense, 2002, pp. 41–2.

20. See on this A. Sharon, *Warrior*, 2nd ed., New York, NY, Simon & Schuster, 2001, pp. 40–50.

21. See, most recently, E. Oren and Y. Bendman, "Iraqi Involvement in the Yom Kippur War", in S. Shai, ed., *The Iraqi-Israeli Conflict*, pp. 72–104.

22. Figures from A. Rotem, "The Next War", in A. Hareven, ed., *Approaching the Year 2000: Towards Peace or Another War?*, Jerusalem, Van Leer, 1988, p. 128.

23. On relations between the three countries during that period see L. A. Brand, "Economics and Shifting Alliances: Jordan's Relations with Syria and Iraq", *International Journal of Middle Eastern Studies*, 26, 1994, pp. 393–413.

24. E. Zeira, *The October 73 War: Myth Against Reality* [Hebrew], Tel Aviv, Yediot Achronot, 1993, pp. 97–8; Alfred Atherton in Parker, ed., *The October War*, p. 123.

25. See the data in S. Brom and Y. Shapir, *The Middle East Military Balance, 2001–2002*, Tel Aviv, Jafee Center for Strategic Studies, 2002, pp. 143–62.

26. Brom and Shapir, *The Middle East Military Balance*, p. 144; see also M. Eisenstadt, "Living with a Nuclear Iran?" *Survival*, 4, 3, autumn 1999, p. 141.

27. See on this M. Eisenstadt, *Iranian Military Power: Capabilities and Intentions*, Washington, D.C., The Washington Institute for Near East Policy, 1996, p. 44.

28. See Brom and Shapir, *The Middle East Military Balance*, pp. 88–9. There is a very detailed quantitative analysis of the balance between the Israeli Air Force and

those of various possible Arab coalitions in Gordon, "Dimensions of Quality", especially chapter 3.

29. http://www.memri.de/uebersetzungen_analysen/laender/aegypten/egypt_mubarak. This refers to a statement made on 6 May 2002. On the way Arab leaders perceive Israeli military power see also Brom and Shapir, *The Middle East Military Balance*, pp. 87–8; and Dowek, *Israeli-Egyptian Relations*, p. 249, which has a long quotation on the subject.

30. See R. Wall, "Interest Balloons in Military Blimps", *Aviation Week*, 11 November 2002, pp. 55–6; J. Flottau, "German Airship Builder Seeks More Funding", *Aviation Week*, 29 April 2002, p. 79.

31. M. Fitzpatrick, "Japan's Blimps Flies High", *New Scientist*, 16 August 2003, p. 7.

32. M. Hewish, "Forces Sharpen Ground Focus", *International Defense Review*, September 2000, p. 53.

33. See I. Tal, *National Security* [Hebrew], Tel Aviv, Dvir, 1996, pp. 221–3. For a discussion, see Y. Steinitz, "The Sea as Israel's Strategic Depth", *Maarachot*, 383, May 2002, pp. 6–11; also, in brief form, "Israel Weighs Expanding Navy to Protect its Nukes", World Tribune.com, 7.11.2002.

34. "The Naval Arm, 2000: Challenge and Response", *Maarachot*, 368, December 1999, pp. 30–5.

35. *The Battle for Peace*, p. 154.

36. For a short acccount see L. Freedman, ed., *The Revolution in Strategic Affairs*, London, IISS, Adelphi Paper No. 318, 1999; also W. Owens, *Lifting the Fog of War*, New York, NY, Farrar, Strauss and Giroux, 2000, especially pp. 97–149.

37. For a more detailed explanation of how this might be done see S. L. Gordon, *The Bow of Paris* [Hebrew], Tel Aviv, Sifriyat Hapoalim, 1997, especially pp. 149–209.

38. The artillery systems in question are described in E. H. Hooton, "Rolling Out the Big Guns", *Jane's Navy International*, January-Feburary 2002, pp. 22–7.

39. See <http://www.boeing.com/phantom/ucav.html>; also D. Glade, "Unmanned Aerial Vehicles: Implications for Military Operations", Occasional Paper No. 16, Center for Strategy and Technology, Maxwell Air Force Base, AL, 2000, p. 12.

40. "The Future of Tactical Aviation", A. Krepinevich testimony to the Senate Armed Services AirLand Subcommittee, 10 March 1999, available at <http://www/csbaonline.org/4Publications/Archive.T.199990310.The_Futu.../T.19990310. The_Future_Of/Tactic.ht>.

41. For a short, state-of-the-art survey of such defenses see A. F. Bloemen and R. R. Wittberg, "Anti-Air Warfare Research for Naval Forces", *Naval Forces*, 21, May 2000, pp. 20–4; and G. Palozi-Horvath, "Counter Measures and Munitions: Defenders of the Fleet", *ibid*, 21, November 2000, pp. 46–53.

42. For the advantages of basing precision-guided strike munitions at sea, as opposed to the land, see O. R. Cote, Jr., "Precision Strike from the Sea: New Missions for a New Navy", Conference Report, MIT, 8–9/12/1997, <www.publications@confseries.strike>.

43. For the possibilities of UAV and UCAV technology now under development see W. B. Scott, "UAV's/UCAVs Finally Join Air Combat Teams", *Aviation Week and Space Technology*, 8.7.2002.

44. See J. C. Toomay, "Technical Characteristics" in R. K. Betts, ed., *Cruise Missiles: Technology, Strategy, Politics*, Washington, D.C., Brookings, 1981, pp. 31–52.

45. See M. Hewish and C. Gilson, "Cruise Context", *International Defense Review*, September 2001, pp. 50–7.

46. See <www.scifitoday.com/story/2003/1/4/7149/84188>.

47. R. Wall, "Tactical Tomahawk Completes First Flight", *Aviation Week*, 2 September 2002, pp. 46–7.

48. See D. A. Fulghum, "Directed-Energy Weapons To Arm Unmanned Craft", *Aviation Week*, 25.2.2002.

49. See, for the details, B. Berkowitz, *The New Face of War*, New York, NY, Free Press, 2003, pp. 122–3.

50. See D. Glade, "Unmanned Aerial Vehicles", p. 18.

51. See, for the rest of this paragraph, D. A. Fulghum and R. Wall, "Israel Pursues High Tech Despite War Costs", *Aviation Week*, 24 June 2002, pp. 78–81; *idem*, "Israel's Future Includes Armed, Long-Range UAV", *ibid*, 24 June 2002, pp. 82–3.

52. D. A. Fulghum and R. Wall, "Small UAVs Built for Use from Large UAVs, Missiles", *Aviation Week*, 22 July 2002, pp. 192–3; R. Wall, "Force Protection UAVs Advance", *ibid*, 26 August 2002, pp. 33–4.

53. For the advantages and disadvantages of an approach based on declaring a casus belli see Horowitz, "Israel's Concept of Defensible Borders", pp. 22–4.

54. This refers to the Grumman AN/APY-3 MTI/SAR radar; Hewish, "Forces Sharpen Ground Focus", p. 51.

55. S. Sadeh, "Night Pilots" [Hebrew], *Air Force Magazine*, 108, April 1996, p. 20.

56. For a fairly detailed description of how it might be done, backed by field exercises, see J. B. Witsken, "Integrating Tactical UAVs Into Armor and Cavalry Operations", *Armor*, March-April 2003, pp. 36–9.

57. According to Gordon, *Israel Against Terror*, p. 66.

58. See, above all, H. Cobban, *The Israeli-Syrian Peace Talks, 1991–96 and Beyond*, Washington, D.C., United States Institute of Peace Press, 1999, pp. 88–9, 91–3, 96–9.

59. A. Ben, "Such Are the Security Arrangements Israel will Demand in Return for Withdrawing from the Golan", *Haaretz*, 19 September 1999, p. B 3.

60. See G. M. Steinberg, "Possible Security Arrangements in the Golan", in Maoz, ed., *The Golan: Between War and Peace* [Hebrew], Or Yehuda, 1999, p. 130.

61. Shalev, *Israel and Syria*, p. 136.

62. See on this Th. K. Adams, "Future Warfare and the Decline of Human Decision-making", *Parameters*, xxxi, 4, winter 2001–2, pp. 57–71.

63. "Israel and Romania Develop Latest Dual-Caliber Multiple Rocket Launcher", *International Defense Review,* 7/2000, p. 11.

64. "Rabin Was Willing to Return Golan", Arab News.com, 29 August 1997. This item is supposedly based on an interview with former U.S. Secretary of State Warren Christopher. A former student of mine, Mr. A. Bregman of London, claims he got the same answer from Christopher.

65. See, however, Shalev, *Israel and Syria,* which analyzes the problem in some detail; also, more recently, U. Bar Yosef, "Israel's Northern Eyes and Shield: The Strategic Value of the Golan Heights Revisited", *Journal of Strategic Studies,* 21, 3, September 1998, pp. 46–66.

66. *Service Record,* I, p. 83.

6. AIRCRAFT, MISSILES, AND WMDS

1. See on this G. Kemp and J. Pressman, *Point of No Return: The Deadly Struggle for Middle East Peace,* Washington, D.C., Carnegie Endowment for International Peace, 1997, pp. 89–90, 198, 207–9.

2. See on this most recently S. Aronson, "Israel's Nuclear Programme, the Six Day War and Its Ramifications", King's College London Mediterranean Studies, London, King's College, 1999, particularly pp. 28–55.

3. See on these problems M. van Creveld, *Nuclear Proliferation and the Future of Conflict,* New York, NY, Free Press, 1993, chapter iv.

4. See, for a short summary, G. Kemp and R. E. Harkavy, *Strategic Geography and the Changing Middle East,* Washington, D.C., Brookings Institution, 1997, pp. 270–83, 381–94.

5. See on this van Creveld, *Nuclear Proliferation,* p. 111.

6. M. Heikal, *Autumn of Fury,* New York, NY, Random House, 1983, p. 180; Al Anba'a [Arabic], Cairo, 15 March 1987.

7. For an Egyptian view on these questions see H. Frisch, "Guns and Butter in the Egyptian Army", in B. Rubin and Th. A. Kearney, eds., *Armed Forces in the Middle East: Politics and Strategy,* London, Cass, 2002, pp. 96–7.

8. See on this D. Shoham, "Chemical Weapons in Egypt and Syria: Development, Capabilities and Arms Control", [Hebrew], *Studies in Middle Eastern Security,* No. 43, Ramat Gan, BEZA Center, 1995, pp. 30–4.

9. Hafez Assad interview, *Newsweek,* 5 August 1991, p. 16–7.

10. See G. Andreani, "Dirty Laundry in Baghdad", *Survival,* 41, 4, winter 1999–2000, p. 169.

11. See e.g. K. Clark, "Afghanistan Faces the Return of the Taliban", *Malaysiakini,* 15 April 2003, available at <http://www.malaysiakini.com/foreignnews/2003041501 11046662989.php>

12. For the background to Iran's nuclear program and the dangers that it does, or does not, pose see Eisenstadt, "Living with a Nuclear Iran?", pp. 125–48.

13. "Musharraf Hits the Israel Button", *Asia Times Online,* 30 June 2003.

14. See on this *The Middle East Military Balance,* 2001–2.

15. For the latest on this see S. G. Stolberg, "Group Says Iran Has Two Undisclosed Nuclear Laboratories", *New York Times,* 27 May 2003.

16. See for example, S. Rodan, "MK Elul Says Israel, U.S. Have Known of Iranian Nukes For Years," *Jerusalem Post,* 4/12/98, [Online] http://www.jpost.co.il. This source credited Iran with four bombs.

17. On the latest concerning Iran see P. Hafezi, "Iran Completes Tests on Missile That Can Hit Israel", Yahoo News, 7 July 2003.

18. G. Douhet, *The Command of the Air,* New York, NY, Arno, 1972 [1921], pp. 18–9.

19. See on this E. C. Dolman, *Astropolitik: Classical Geopolitics in the Space Age,* London, Cass, 2002.

20. See on this B. G. Blair, *Strategic Command and Control,* Washington, D.C., Brookings, 1985, pp. 140–7.

21. For some figures on this question see S. J. Rosen, "Military Geography and the Military Balance in the Arab-Israel Conflict", Jerusalem Papers on Peace Problems, Jerusalem, The Hebrew University, 1977, p. 10 table I.

22. President Bush has ordered his intelligence services to get as many of their images as they can from commercial suppliers; J. Bamford, "Big Brother is Tracking You without a Warrant", *New York Times,* 18 May 2003 (Internet edition).

23. *The Battle for Peace,* p. 215. See also Gordon, "Dimensions of Quality", p. 85 figure 20, who argues that the Arab-Israeli balance of power in the air is relatively insensitive to changes in the infrastructure.

24. Missile Defense News Update, 3 May 2003, available at <http://www.clw.org/nmd/nmdupdates/030305.html>; "Taiwan Military Deploying Missile Defense Network", People's News Daily, 6 March 2003, available at <http://english.peopledaily. com.cn/>.

25. <http/usinfo.state.gov/topical/pol/arms/02122203.html.>.

26. Dr. Uzi Landau, "Ballistic Missile Defense", in A. Stav, ed., *Ballistic Missiles—Threat and Response* [Hebrew], Tel Aviv, Yediot Achronot, 2000, p. xvi; also F. Gafni, "The Aegis Option", *ibid,* pp. 220–1.

27. J. J. Tcakik, "Taiwan: Concerned Western Action Could Supply Subs", *Defense News Weekly,* 16 September 2002.

28. See on this J. C. Anselemo, "U.S. Seen More Vulnerable to Electromagnetic Attack", *Aviation Week,* 28 July 1997, p. 67.

29. For a thorough, if somewhat old, discussion of this topic see S. Feldman, *Israeli Nuclear Deterrence,* New York, NY, Columbia University Press 1982, pp. 54–61. Also, more recently, U. Bar Yosef, "Variations on a Theme: The Conceptualization of Deterrence in Israeli Strategic Thinking", *Security Studies,* 7, 3, spring 1998, particularly pp. 155–81.

30. See e.g. Y. Dror. *Crazy States: A Counterconventional Strategic Problem,* Lexington, MA, Lexington Books, 1971.

31. See on this, most recently, Busheri, "The Security Concept of Yigal Allon as Compared to that of Ben Gurion", pp. 10, 128–54.

32. See on this H. Goodman and W. Seth Carus, *The Future Battlefield and the Arab-Israeli Conflict,* New Brunswick, NJ, Transaction, 1990, especially p. 116.

33. The respective dates are 1985 (when two Syrian planes were downed over Lebanon) and 1982.

34. Mohammad Heikal, 1996, as quoted in E. Lerman, "Israel's Strategic Environment in the Post-Cold War Age", in Golan, ed., *Israel's Security Web,* p. 168.

35. A. Levite and E. B. Landau, *Israel's Nuclear Image: Arab Prospects of Israel's Nuclear Weapons,* Tel Aviv, Tel Aviv University, 1994, p. 111.

36. Eisenstadt, "Living with a Nuclear Iran?", p. 135.

37. This is also the figure mentioned by R. Bergman, "IDF: Preparing for an Iranian Atom Bomb in 2005", *Yediot Achronot,* Weekend Supplement, 8 August 2003, p. 5.

38. See on this F. Barnaby, *The Invisible Bomb: The Nuclear Arms Race in the Middle East,* London, Tauris, 1989, p. 25, which is based on the Vanunu revelations; see also Lt. Col. "S", "The Nuclear Threat against Israel", *Maarachot,* 386, November 2002, p. 8; Wm. Robert Johnston, "Nuclear Warheads and Applications", September 2000, available at <www.johnstonsarchive.net/nuclear/wrjp159z/html>.

39. G. Ben Dor, "Arab Rationality and Deterrence", in A. Klieman and A. Levite, eds., *Deterrence in the Middle East: Where Theory and Practice Converge,* Boulder, CO, Westview, 1993, p. 88.

40. See on this E. Karsh, "Rational Ruthlessness: Non-Conventional and Missile Warfare in the Iran-Iraq War", in E. Karsh and others, eds., *Non-Conventional Weapons Proliferation in the Middle East,* Oxford, Clarendon, 1993, pp. 31–48.

41. *Haaretz,* 4, 5, 6 April 1990; *Al Ahali* [Arabic], 16 May 1990.

42. Bass, *Support Any Friend,* p. 193.

43. See A. Baram, "Saddam Hussein", in Shai, ed., *The Iraqi-Israeli Conflict,* pp. 139–58.

44. Quoted in "Ron", "Surface to Surface Missile Activity during the Gulf War", in Shai, ed., *The Iraqi-Israeli Conflict,* p. 168.

45. See, however, Inbar and Sandler, "Israel's Deterrence Strategy Revisited", *Security Studies,* 3, 2, pp. 331–6.

7. BROADER HORIZONS

1. See on this Peri, "The Israeli Military and Israel's Palestinian Policy", p. 30.

2. Arian, *Security Threatened,* p. 26 figure 2.1.

3. For a good summary of the former position see S. Peres, *The New Middle East,* New York, NY, Holt, 1993, pp. 1–60; for the latter, Sohar, *A Concubine in the Middle East,*

pp. 207–19; see also Th. Friedman. *From Beirut to Jerusalem,* London, Collins, 1990, pp. 520–1.

4. Quoted in Y. Cohen, *By Light and by Darkness,* Tel Aviv, Am Oved, 1969, p. 274.

5. N. Machiavelli, *The Prince,* Harmondsworth, Middlesex, Penguin ed., 1969, pp. 95–106. Machiavelli's rules are: 1. Strike so hard that you won't have to strike twice; 2. Do whatever you have to do openly, without apologizing; and 3. Make somebody else do the dirty work so you can disassociate yourself in case of failure.

6. See on this, most recently, O. Shalom, "That's How We Shall Prevent Evacuation", *Yediot Achronot,* Weekend Magazine, 16 May 2003, pp. 10–2.

7. See on this possibility E. Sprinzak, "Extremism and Violence in Israeli Democracy", *Terrorism and Political Violence,* 12, 3–4, autumn/winter 2000, pp. 209–36. Also Y. Levy, *The Other Army of Israel,* p. 387; and Y. Gvirtz, "The Danger—Active Opposition to Evacuation", *Yediot Achronot,* Weekend Magazine, 30 May 2002, pp. 12–3.

8. "Peace Now" poll, reported on Israel TV News Bulletin, 23 July 2003.

9. *Haaretz,* 10 July 2002, pp. A 1, A 6.

10. *Maariv* Finance Magazine, 9 June 2003, p. 1.

11. *Maariv,* 7 August 2003, p. 8.

12. Peace Now poll, Israel TV News Bulletin, 23 July 2003.

13. There used to be two, but one was abolished for reasons of economy. Israel Radio News Bulletin, 28 May 2003.

14. Israel TV News Bulletin, 6 August 2003.

15. IDF Judge Advocate's Report to the Knesset Committee on Law, 22 June 2003, reported in *Yediot Achronot,* 23 June 2003, p. 15.

16. Quoted in *Haaretz,* 10 July 2003, p. A 6.

17. See R. A. Gabriel and P. L. Savage, *Crisis in Command,* New York, NY, Hill & Wang, 1978.

18. See the reservist officers' letter to the minister of defense, published in Ynet, 12 February 2002.

19. Israel TV News Bulletin, 29.10.1996.

20. For the latest on this problem see *Yediot Achronot,* 6.12.2002, p. 2.

21. See on this A. Fishman, "Ya'alon's Five Year Plan", *Yediot Achronot,* Weekend Supplement, 4 July 2003, p. 28.

22. For some thought as to how it might be done see A. Sobelman, "Information on the Modern Battlefield and Information Warfare", in Golan, ed., *Israel's Security Web,* pp. 218–36 also Y. Ben Israel, "Security, Technology and the Future Battlefield", *ibid,* pp. 269–327.

23. What that might mean was spelled out in a lecture by General U. Adam, Commanding Officer, Technology and Logistics Division, IDF, Ramat Gan, Bar Illan University, 14 May 2003.

24. More details in *Aviation Week*, 24 June 2002, p. 79; also D. Eshel, "The Merkava Mk 4", *Armor*, January-February 2003, pp. 4–6.

25. See S. L. Myers, "Army Is Restructuring with Brigades for Rapid Response", *New York Times*, 13 October 1999; R. Suro, "Chief Projects Army on Wheels", *Washington Post*, 13 October 1999.

26. For a discussion of how this might be done see Y. Lifschitz, "Managing Defense After 2000", in H. Golan, ed., *Israel's Security Web*, pp. 57–63; also S. L. Gordon, "In Favor of Selective Service", *Maarachot*, 328, January-February 1993, pp. 32–7; and Levy, *The Other Army of Israel*, p. 462.

27. See on this M. van Creveld, *Technology and War, From 2000 B.C. to the Present*, New York, NY, Free Press, 1989, p. 272.

8. CONCLUSIONS

1. Frisch, "Guns and Butter in the Egyptian Army", pp. 99,101–2.

2. See e.g. the detailed analysis in D. Shoham, "Chemical and Biological Weapons in Arab and Iranian Hands—An Existential Threat to Israel?" [Hebrew], *Studies in Middle Eastern Security*, No.43, Ramat Gan, BEZA Center, 1999.

3. Israel Radio News Bulletin, 31 July 2003.

4. For some of the latest on this see P. Krugman, "Denial and Deception", *New York Times*, 24 June 2002; "Majority in U.S. Believes Bush Stretched Truth about Iraq", Yahoo! News, 3 July 2003. Not to be outdone, the Knesset Committee on Defense Foreign Affairs is also looking into the question; Israel Radio News Bulletin, 24 June 2003.

5. Concerning nuclear weapons see A. Koch and J. Wolf, "Iran's Nuclear Procurement Program: How Close Is It to the Bomb?", *The Nonproliferation Review*, Fall 1997, p. 133; concerning missiles, S. Rodan, "Secret Israeli Data Reveals Iran Can Make Missile in a Year". *Defense News*, 6–12 October 1997.

6. See A. Cordesman, *Iran and Iraq: The Threat from the Northern Gulf*, Boulder, CO, Westview, 1996, p. 108.

7. *Yediot Achronot*, 30 January 1995.

8. See on this van Creveld, *The Sword and the Olive*, pp. 273–4.

9. For some worst-case scenarios see E. Inbar and S. Sandler, "The Risks of Palestinian Statehood", *Mideast Security and Policy Studies*, No. 33, Ramat Gan, Begin-Sadat Center for Strategic Studies, 1997.

10. PLO figures: quoted from Efrat, *Geography of Occupation*, p. 139.

11. See, however, M. de Villiers, *Water: The Fate of Our Most Precious Resource*, Boston, MA, Houghton Miflin, 2001, pp. 188–203; and, at greater length, S. D. Kiser, *The Hydraulic Parameter of Conflict in the Middle East and North Africa*, Colorado Springs, CO, INSS, 2000, pp. 1–35.

12. A. Zarchin statement, available at <http://www.bway.net/~epic/AlexanderZarchin.html>. More figures on the extent of the problem and the possibility of solving it

by way of the desalination and recycling of water are available in Efrat, *Geography of Occupation*, p. 78–9.

13. J. Schwarz, "Water Resources Development and Management in Israel", in B. Rubin, ed., *Efficient Use of Limited War Resources: Making Israel a Model State*, Ramat Gan, BEZA Center, 2001, p. 81.

14. According to A. Soffer, "Mapping Special Interest Groups in Israel's Water Policy", in Rubin, ed., *Efficient Use of Limited Water Resources*, p. 139.

15. The phrase comes from Zeev Jabotinsky, great-grandfather of today's Likud; see A. Shlaim, *The Iron Wall; Israel and the Arab World*, New York, NY, Norton, 2000, pp. 12–6.

16. Speech of 6.3.1981, in M. Dayan, *On the Peace Process and the Future of Israel* [Hebrew], N. Yanai, ed., Tel Aviv, Ministry of Defense, p. 254.